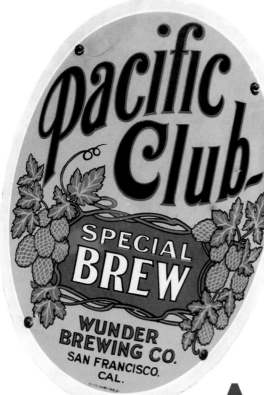

More Porcelain Enamel Advertising

Michael Bruner

4880 Lower Valley Road, Atglen, PA 19310

Dedication

For my mother, Bernadine Bruner.

Bruner, Michael, 1952-
    More porcelain enamel advertising / Michael Bruner.
        p.   cm.
    ISBN 0-7643-0373-2 (paper)
    1. Advertising--Collectibles--United States--Catalogs. 2. Enamel
signs and signboards--Collectors and collecting--United States--Catalogs.
3. Decorative arts--United States--History--19th century--Catalogs. 4.
Decorative arts--United States--History--20th century--Catalogs. I.
Title.
NK6511.S53B79   1997
659.13'42--dc21   97-19062
                                                                CIP

Copyright © 1997 by Mike Bruner

1 2 3 4   Book Layout by Blair Loughrey

                    ISBN: 0-7643-0373-2
                    Printed in Hong Kong

Published by Schiffer Publishing Ltd.
4880 Lower Valley Road
Atglen, PA 19310
Phone: (610) 593-1777; Fax: (610) 593-2002
E-mail: Schiffer@aol.cpm
Please write for a free catalog.
This book may be purchased from the publisher.
Please include $3.95 for shipping.
Try your bookstore first.

We are interested in hearing from authors
with book ideas on related subjects.

Special Thanks and Acknowledgements

As with any worthwhile endeavor, certain key people made a lot of difference in how smoothly this book went together. The enthusiasm extended toward myself and this project in general has given me the ability to take the initial germ of a book idea to the fruition of this finished volume. I'd like to especially thank the following people for going the extra mile and contributing their special talents toward this second book on porcelain enamel advertising.

To Peter Schiffer, my publisher, my sincere appreciation for your support throughout this project.

To Sharon Callender and the crew at Drayton Printing and Copy Center, for your assistance with text layout.

To Shawn David, my sincere thanks for your support and help in the production stages.

To Donna Salzman, who chauffeured me on a 900-mile, one-day photo trip through California's deserts and mountains.

To Red Sonnen, my sincere appreciation for your efforts on several of my books. Oh, by the way, thanks to you too, Gene.

To John R. Heafield at PHOTOFAST, Birmingham, Michigan, whose photofinishing is used in the majority of my photographic work.

My sincere appreciation,
Mike Bruner

Contributors

The following is an alphabetical listing of contributors who shared their time and allowed me to photograph items for the book. Some individuals asked to remain anonymous, and their contributions are much appreciated.

John Alinder, Leseur, Minnesota
David Belcher, San Antonio, Texas
Crockett Blacklock, Redwood Valley, California
Roger Blad, Burnsville, Minnesota
Tim and Leevona Blair, Harrisonville, Missouri
Blumenthal's, Greensboro, North Carolina
John Bobroff, Running Spring, California
Bill and Karen Brown, Ochelata, Oklahoma
Dale Brown, Great Bend, Kansas
Buck Signs, Mifflinburg, Pennsylvania
Layne Christensen, Eden, Utah
Cips Sign in Mt. Sterling, Illinois
Columbus, Wisconsin
Country Charm Antiques, Stillwater, Minnesota
Tom and Susan Dahl, Minneapolis, Minnesota
Shawn David, Waterford, Michigan
DeZalia & Sons Garage, Severance, New York
Eagle Signs, Reynoldsville, Pennsylvania
Sam Ezell, Daniel Boone Village, Hillsboro, North
    Carolina
Frank Feher, West Sacramento, California
Joe Pete Forcer, Baird, Texas
Fox & Hounds Antique Mall, Myrtle Beach, South
    Carolina
Bill and Belinda Fraser, Cumming, Georgia
Gardnerville, Nevada
Kelley Hasselback, Charlotte, Michigan
Henneburg, Parkersburg, West Virginia
Mick Hoover, Mackay, Idaho
Harold and Donna Huddleston, Denton, Texas
I.F.C.A. at Fenton, Michigan
Debbie Jackson, Blaine, Minnesota
George Jacques, at Adirondack & Rustic Furnishings,
    Keene Valley, New York
Steve Jones, Minneapolis, Minnesota
Pete Keim, Sunnyvale, California

Kendalls Barn, Chester, Vermont
Kim and Mary Kokles, Dallas, Texas
Lee and Bonnie Kollorz, Vacaville, California
Rod Krupka, Ortonville, Michigan
Dave and Kathy Lane, Tulsa, Oklahoma
Tom Licouris, Fresno, California
Don Mangells, Catoosa, Oklahoma
Dick Marrah, Sacramento, California
Richard Merriman, Radnor, Pennsylvania
Gary Metz, Roanoake, Virginia
Jerry and Phyllis Miller, Hunta, Ontario, Canada
More Antiques, Stillwater, Minnesota
Motel Sign, near San Jose, Illinois
Robert Newman, Los Angeles, California
Jim Oswald, Bountiful, Utah
Pam at Parkside Antique Mall, Princeton, Wisconsin
Steve Parker, Rexburg, Idaho
Princine Petinga, Bloomfield Hills, Michigan
Dick and Kathy Purvis, Manchester, Connecticut
Vic and Sara Raupe, Guthrie, Oklahoma
Ron Raymer at Rusty Relicks, Russell, Kansas
Randy Reith, VanBuren, Arkansas
Reno, Nevada
W.K. Richards, Raleigh, North Carolina
John Romagnoli, Fresno, California
John Rutske, Bloomington, Minnesota
Schooltime Antiques, Earl, Wisconsin
Larry Schrof, Geneseo, Illinois
Jeffery Ingram Sherill, Dalton, Georgia
Gene and Red Sonnen, St. Paul, Minnesota
Terry Stady, Albuquerque, New Mexico
Steve Stromski, Westland, Michigan
Darryl Tilden, Minneapolis, Minnesota
Rick Trotnic, Parsons, Kansas
Ernie Vigil, Aptos, California
Michael Villamagna, Franklin, Ohio
Tom and Sherry Watt, Glyndon, Minnesota
Denis and Jeanie Weber, St. Joseph, Missouri
Wendall White, Centerville, Utah
Chuck Witte, Oklahoma City, Oklahoma

Contents

Preface 6

Introduction 7

Estimating a Sign's Age 8

Grading Condition 9

Repaired Signs 10

Chapter 1
Petroleum & Automobile Signs 11

Chapter Two
Flat One- and Two-Sided Signs 47

Chapter Three
Flanged Two-Sided Signs 89

Chapter Four
Curved Signs 102

Chapter Five
Thermometers, Door Pushes,
Trays, & Smalls 111

Chapter Six
A Porcelain Potpourri 129

Chapter Seven
Ingram-Richardson, A Photo Essay 139

Parting Shots 159

Preface

The past few years have seen a tremendous growth in collecting antique advertising. Of the many media used by companies to bring attention to their products or services, none seem to have had the overall appeal of porcelain enamel. The process of creating porcelain signs is an art in itself, and the influx of new collectors in the marketplace attests to porcelain enamel advertising's beauty. Few collectibles are made with such long-lasting properties or have been found in such diversity as porcelain enamel advertising.

For all the magnificent designs that have turned up through the years, it is of interest to note that the hobby of collecting this advertising is of relatively recent vintage. Possibly collectors couldn't see the forest for the trees! So many times we have been bombarded with advertising in our everyday life that we really paid little attention to such matter-of-fact items. I've been to many places that had some type of porcelain sign outside the building, only to find out the owner had no idea that the advertising sign I mentioned was on the premises!

Like so many other collectibles, the stimulus for collecting porcelain enamel advertising was that it was no longer being manufactured, and it is gradually disappearing from the eye of the general public. The past few years have seen the removal of most of the remaining porcelain enamel signs that were still "in use." Normally, a long search will not turn up anything but the most common pieces still doing service. With little porcelain advertising to be found in its original place, those wanting a piece of the action must now turn to the collectors' market to build a collection.

The heartbeat of any hobby is the ability to buy, sell, or trade. Collecting porcelain advertising is certainly no different in that it's the people in the hobby that make it an enjoyable experience. It is possible to build a fine collection by staying at home, writing letters, making phone calls, etcetera. However, to really network yourself, it pays to attend shows. Many dealers are specialists in advertising, and come up with some pretty unusual items. A few shows throughout the country even specialize in advertising, and a good mix of porcelain advertising will usually be present. These shows are generally well advertised in the major antique publications. Don't get discouraged by the fact that some of the pieces you want for your collection are not available. Patience will almost always pay off in the long run. And as far as prices go, if you like it and you can afford it, then buy it! I've been involved in several hobbies through the years, and in my judgment, porcelain advertising does appreciate in value over time. This is especially true on the better items.

As you go through this book, you can't help but notice the tremendous degree of diversity that can be found in porcelain advertising. Not only signs, but dozens of other everyday items were made with a porcelain message. Keep in mind that you are only looking at the tip of the iceberg. There were thousands of porcelain signs manufactured in this country during the last hundred years. However, due to World War II's scrap effort, possibly as few as thirty percent of the total signs manufactured have survived. Despite this seemingly discouraging view, there are endless possibilities for new finds in basements, attics, bulk plants, and defunct manufacturing facilities. Proof of this can be seen at antique advertising shows, with a never-ending stream of new discoveries coming through the door.

This volume will give you an idea of the beauty and diverse graphics to be found in this very collectible area of Americana.

I look forward to hearing from you. Please feel free to write to me c/o 4103 Lotus Drive, Waterford, Michigan 48329.

Mike Bruner

Introduction

To help us understand how porcelain enamel advertising came into collectible status, a brief understanding of its day-to-day use is helpful. As the art of porcelain enamel production was perfected, it became an inexpensive way for a business to promote its products. By the turn of the century, porcelain enamel advertising became so commonplace that few merchants could be found who weren't displaying some type of porcelain sign. No longer was porcelain advertising a luxury. It became the standard by which to judge all other advertising forms.

As the years progressed, so did the imaginations of those responsible for creating the signs. Square and rectangular signs gave way to "die-cut" designs, new effort was put into the color schemes, and anything and everything was tried. This kept manufacturers busy for the better part of the century.

In time, though, many manufacturers went by the wayside. The smaller firms could not compete. The rising costs involved in the production of porcelain enamel made many businesses consider alternative methods of advertising. This spelled doom for sign manufacturers. By the 1970s, the production of porcelain enamel advertising became a closed chapter in American history.

The good news is that collectors have recognized porcelain enamel as an important connection to the past. It is a link to the products and services that made this country great. Unfortunately, some of the companies that advertised in porcelain are no longer with us, but many are still around, possibly owing to the porcelain advertising they used throughout the years.

The products to be found advertised in porcelain are almost endless. As you read through the book, you will see the wide range of advertisers who used this medium. There seem to be certain subjects that received more of the advertising market than others, particularly products or services that were frequently used by the public. Leading the list would be petroleum signs, and any advertising relating to the automobile or gasoline. It would be safe to say that there was more petroleum-related porcelain enamel advertising produced than there was in any other category. I've reserved Chapter One exclusively for these items. Many collectors specialize in "petro" advertising and find the number of items produced over the years nearly endless. Other companies to make heavy use of porcelain advertising were manufacturers of beer, paints and varnishes, telephones, tobacco, and soda pop.

As a collector, don't make the mistake of trying to acquire everything. If you want to collect by the pound, that is fine; but keep in mind how much is out there! It's just not practical to think that you can collect everything that was produced. Instead, set your sights on a more realistic approach. One of the most common would be to specialize in a certain company or product. One collector I know collects only blue and white porcelain, and he says it goes great with his graniteware! Possibly a special interest in your personal life will find its way to your collection. As an example, I know several people who are telephone company employees that specialize in porcelain telephone advertising. After a brief period you'll find out what it is that interests you.

You will find this book divided into several chapters. Each chapter covers items by manufacturing design or subject matter. Each photograph will have a brief description plus any relevant comments, the sign's measurements—width first, then height -- and a value estimate. Also, the approximate age of the items will be given. Please keep in mind that estimating the age of a sign is done by using a combination of several techniques. These are covered in a separate section in the book.

For those of you privileged enough to have lived in the era of porcelain advertising, get ready for a trip down memory lane. And for those of us that wish to go back to a time we never saw, the following pages will provide a vivid portrait of our past in porcelain enamel advertising.

Estimating a Sign's Age

Very few porcelain signs have been made with the date of manufacture or intended use on them. The most notable exception to this would be Coca-Cola signs that had their manufacturing date ink-stamped on them. Most of these date to the 1930s. Some automobile signs have been found with the year of their service on them as well. For the most part, a sign's age cannot be pinpointed without a date right on the sign. There are, however, some techniques that can be helpful in determining the approximate age of a sign.

The most scholastic method requires that the name of the manufacturer be on the sign. If this information is known, then some research can tell you the dates during which the company was in business. This may not in itself accomplish much, because many companies were producing signs for decades. If the street address of the manufacturer is on the sign you might get a better idea of the sign's age, because many times a company only operated at a particular address for a brief time. These methods take some real knowledge of the companies that were in business, and you might spend considerable time researching this information.

Another approach would be to size up the product advertised. This means that if you know the history of the product or service advertised on the sign, you can use this information to help you determine the sign's age. For example, if you found a Mobilgas sign with the Pegasus logo on it, you would know that the age of the sign was later than the 1920s. Mobil did not use the Pegasus logo until the 1930s. Similarly, if you guessed that a Brazil Beer sign dates to the 1940s, you would be considerably off, as this company was doing business during the first years of the century.

Although these methods are helpful, using them requires a knowledge of the products being advertised.

There is another method that seems to work even better.

The most accepted and reliable method of dating a sign is the look and feel of the porcelain. Most of the older signs—those dating before 1930—were made using a stencil. This technique always produced a bumpy feel at the edges where different colors meet. Called "shelving," it was caused by the firing of more than one coat of porcelain. Some signs were fired five or six times, leaving a pronounced shelving effect. Normally a sign made after 1940 will not have a high degree of this layered feel.

As unusual as this may seem, the back side of sign may tell you more than the front. A porcelain coat will normally be found on the back side. The color of this coating can range from a light gray to a bluish-black and everything in between. The oldest signs will have many small spots where there is no porcelain. Some signs may have over a hundred of these small spots. This would indicate a sign of pre 1930 vintage, as manufacturers used methods that eliminated most of these spots after that time. This technique is for signs with the advertising on only one side.

A high degree of hand production work is evident on older signs. It is common to find fingerprints fired right into the porcelain, sometimes in two or more colors! Once in a while you will find a set of numbers finger written and fired into the porcelain. Let's say, as an example, that you find the number "3-07." You could assume that the sign in your hands was manufactured in March of 1907.

As you gain experience as a collector, you will find your ability to estimate a sign's age has improved. Talking with other collectors is helpful. Much can be quickly learned from their knowledge.

Grading Condition

The increased use of the mail and the telephone for buying and selling antique advertising has created a need to develop a standard grading scale. Condition on a piece is of extreme importance when buying a sign sight unseen. In the past there have been some problems in grading. By using the grading scale in this book, it is hoped that these problems will be minimized.

In describing a sign, the seller must make an accurate assessment of damage. The buyer expects to have no surprises when the sign arrives, and if it has been graded correctly the buyer will be inclined to follow through with the transaction.

The majority of signs in "collectible" condition fall into the grading scale between a rating of 6 and 10. Those pieces that are below Grade 6 have lost enough of their eye appeal to be of limited interest. To get a more accurate guide to condition, a value can be expressed in decimal points. As an example, to grade a sign between 8 and 9 we would grade it an "8.5." This universally accepted system of grading offers better understanding than using terms such as mint, near mint, very good, good, et cetera.

The following descriptions should help you grade porcelain enamel signs.

Grade 10: Like new, out-of-the-box condition. Eyelets, if any, can show use or be missing, but no chips can be around the eyelet holes.

Grade 9.5: Very close to like-new condition with original luster to the porcelain but with a slight amount of damage, such as small screw hole chips, light scratches or a small chip to non-critical sections of the image area. Small edge nicks in limited numbers may be found.

Grade 9.0: Small areas of edge damage that do not detract from the overall appearance of the advertising. Several small or one larger edge chip are acceptable. Porcelain gloss should be intact, but the surface may show slight signs of use. The image area may have a small chip.

Grade 8.5: Chips become more numerous or may go into some of the image area. There may be slight loss of luster to part of the porcelain. Edge damage becomes more prominent, but does not detract from the overall appearance.

Grade 8.0: The image area may have a small amount of damage that will detract somewhat, but this will be confined to a minimum. There can be surface scratches or loss of luster. Damage outside the image area is more pronounced, with many edge chips or larger size chips to the screw holes or the flange area.

Grade 7.5: More noticeable damage to the sign with several large-size chips. The porcelain may have loss of luster in some areas and surface scratches could detract somewhat. Chips in the image area will be present, but will not be so large that a significant amount of eye-appeal is lost. Flange damage could be extensive.

Grade 7.0: Chipping is more pronounced, with many edge chips and several chips in the image area. There may be chips in a critical area of the image. Much wear could be present with significant loss of porcelain luster and scratches.

Grade 6.0: There is significant loss of eye-appeal, with the image area damaged considerably. Several larger size chips will be present, and flange damage could be severe.

Keep in mind that on flanged signs and signs that have an image area on both sides, a grade must be established for each side. Manufacturer's defects will occasionally be present and although they are not considered damage, they should be mentioned.

As a rule, all chips are not created equal. Edge chips are not as significant as the same size chips would be on the inside area. Normally the edge area is expected to have some damage, and this is not as critical as the center being damaged. The principal question to answer is how much the damage detracts from the appeal of the sign. A 30-inch Conoco minuteman sign in super condition, except that a chip the size of a quarter took out the minuteman's face, will go from a condition of 9.5-plus to around 7.0 simply because few collectors would find a faceless minuteman very attractive. This is especially true at the prices these signs are going for!

If a sign is two-sided, then a grade must be given for each side. If the sign has a flange, mention of the condition should be made, keeping in mind that flange damage is not as critical to a sign's appeal as damage to the face.

As many collectors network with others who share similar interests, it will pay to be as honest and accurate as possible in grading the condition of signs.

Repaired Signs

As prices continue to increase in the market, repairing a sign seems to make good sense. There are times, however, when repairing can be an exercise in futility. The basis for all sign repairs is how the sign will look compared to its appearance before the work was done. The decision is up to the owner. You must ask whether the damage is so unsightly that it's going to make the repair a worthwhile investment. If the answer is no, then it is best to just leave the sign the way it is. If you decide to have repairs made, the next step is to get the job done right.

There are several levels of quality in the sign repair business. "So-so" and "terrible" are the levels most frequently encountered. Unfortunately, most of the sign repairs out there never reach the quality of "great" due to the amateur nature of the work. Anyone can get out a can of body filler and go to town. However, to do professional work requires a lot of practice, and work of truly high quality comes from only a few select craftspeople.

When a sign that is damaged enough to be rated a seven is repaired so that it appears to be a mint condition sign, then you have a quality repair. There are people that can do repairs at this level, but they are expensive and you may not want to make the investment unless it will enhance the sign's value. If you have a sign that has a market value of $300 in mint condition and the repair costs are $275, it might be in your best interest to leave it and invest in a more worthwhile repair. Normally, the higher priced signs will be worth the cost of repairs, provided the workmanship is of high caliber.

How does a repair affect the value of a sign? There are some variables to consider, including the extent of repair on the sign and the quality of the work. On average, though, a sign that had a quality repair job would be worth at least sixty to seventy percent of what the sign would have been worth in mint condition with no repairs. As an example, if a given sign has a market value in mint condition of $1,000, then a sign repaired so that it appears to be in mint condition should be worth at least $650 to $750. Again, it must be emphasized that these figures are for quality repairs only. Home type garage repairs will likely do little to enhance a sign's value, and may even lower it.

In conclusion, the decision to repair a sign is solely that of the owner. However, dealers and collectors selling repaired signs have an ethical responsibility to be up-front and honest about repairs. Having a photo available of the pre-repaired sign has been suggested by numerous collectors.

Chapter 1
Petroleum & Automobile Signs

The signs found in this chapter all relate to the petroleum market. There were thousands of signs manufactured through the years in these categories and they comprise the largest single subject matter found in porcelain enamel advertising. This chapter will contain signs that are flat, one-sided, and two-sided, as well as flanged signs, pump signs, hanging signs, those found in sidewalk lollipop type stands, etcetera.

One of the most outstanding petroleum signs to be found is this Oilzum Motor Oils and Lubricants sign. The man with the hat and its catchy slogan puts it at the top of collectors' most wanted lists. It was made in the 1920s by Ingram Richardson; 24", $2,500. *Courtesy of Bill and Karen Brown.*

Notice the wood grain contained in the outline of the lettering of this graphic, Oak Motor Oil sign; c. 1920s, 24", $1,400. *Courtesy of Dave and Kathy Lane.*

Shell Oil is one of the largest petroleum companies in the world. This Shellubrication sign was manufactured in the 1930s to promote their lubrication services; approximately 5" x 19", $650. *Courtesy of Tom and Susan Dahl.*

Texaco wanted its customers to know that its lubrication methods were approved. This strip sign dates from 1932, as evidenced by the ink-stamped "3-32" at bottom center; 39" x 9", $450. *Courtesy of Mick Hoover.*

The Automobile Dealers of California sponsored a club to service motorists. This flat, two-sided sign was designed to be hung from a bracket; c. 1940s, 14" x 27", $250. *Courtesy of John Bobroff.*

Loyal-Penn was a product of Red Hat Gasoline Corporation. This round sign features the Pennsylvania Oil logo at the top with the Red Hat Royal 400 insignia at the bottom; 28", $1500. *Courtesy of Dave and Kathy Lane.*

Muskegon, Michigan, was home to Musgo Corporation. Although they only served a small market, their legendary round roadside sign has made Musgo a household word for petro collectors. It was made by Veribrite; c. 1930s, 48", $3500. *Courtesy of Dave and Kathy Lane.*

Riley Brothers was a relatively short-lived company producing only oil products; c. 1930s, 26" x 16.5", $300. *Courtesy of John Bobroff.*

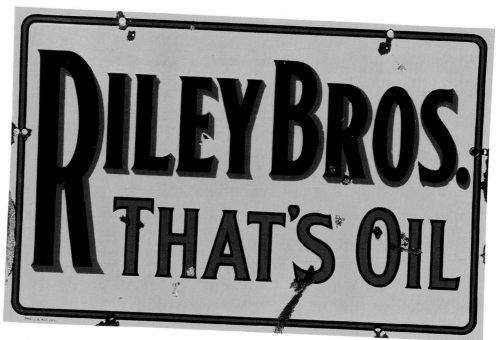

This tombstone-shaped Penn-Veedol Motor Oil sign deviates from their normal orange, black, and white color scheme. It was designed to be mounted on a sidewalk stand; c. 1930s, 22" x 28", $400. *Courtesy of John Bobroff.*

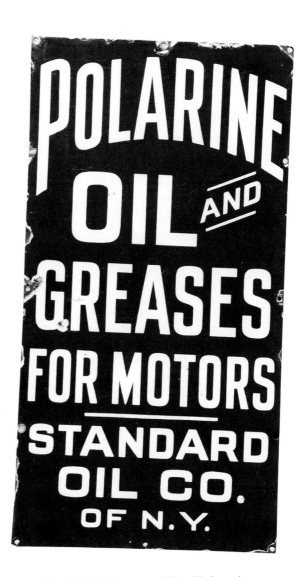

Standard Oil Company of New York used this Polarine Oil and Greases sign in the 1920s; 12" x 22", $300. *Courtesy of John Bobroff.*

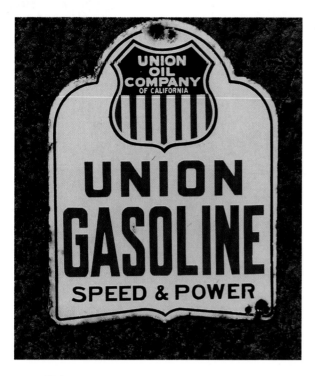

Union Gasoline was a product of Union Oil Company of California; c. 1930s, 12" x 15", $1,500. *Courtesy of John Romagnoli.*

Goodrich Tires produced this Slow Down Guide Post sign as a safety marker near intersections and crosswalks; c. 1920s, 20", $400. *Courtesy of Mick Hoover.*

This Sheldon Oil Company pump sign dates from the 1950s; 16" x 9", $250. *Courtesy of Mick Hoover.*

This curved Golden Texaco Motor Oil sign was designed to be used on a visible gasoline pump, which would date it to the era around 1925-1930; $750. *Courtesy of John Romagnoli.*

The Ethyl Corporation logo was the big feature on this two-sided, 1930s Crystal Gasoline sign; 30", $300. *Courtesy of John Bobroff.*

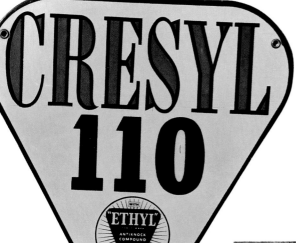

This Cresyl pump sign features a large 110 and the Ethyl logo at the bottom. Although we certainly know what the Ethyl logo told us, could it really be possible that this pump sign advertised a fuel rated at 110 octane? It dates from the 1940s; $350. *Courtesy of John Romagnoli.*

Mohawk Gasoline uses their Indian head logo on this side-mount sign; c. 1920s, $2500. Courtesy of John Romagnoli.

Tens of thousands of license plates were manufactured in the early years of the American automobile. No doubt it became evident that the high cost of production of porcelain enamel was not necessary since license plates were only designated to last one year. As you can see, this Massachusetts plate dating from 1912 lasted a whole lot longer; $200. *Courtesy of Jeffery Ingram Sherill.*

15

Polarine was one of the largest selling motor oils in the world. This sign was manufactured by Ingram Richardson; c. 1920, $400. *Courtesy of Jeffery Ingram Sherill.*

Beacon Oils used this attractive, shield-shaped pump sign around 1930. Although not evident by the photograph, it is made of heavy metal with stenciled porcelain graphics that produced a rather thick porcelain coat; $750. *Courtesy of John Romagnoli.*

Standard Oil Company of California was one of the first petroleum companies to accept purchases on credit. This Red Crown Gasoline Scrip Accepted sign was placed prominently at pump side; c. 1920, $1,500. *Courtesy of John Romagnoli*

Although this Skelly tombstone sign is the center of attention, we must not overlook the outstanding embossed base found below. These are quite rare and make a good sign even better; $850. *Courtesy of Ron Raymer.*

This beautiful Hancock No Smoking Stop Motor strip sign dates from the 1920s; $850. *Courtesy of John Romagnoli.*

Although the condition of this McCandless Mazda Automobile Lamps sign is less than perfect, its outstanding graphics, which differ on each side, warrant its proper place in history. If the heavy-gauge metal with thick porcelain isn't enough to convince you of its age, the two children in an early vehicle should help you date this one to about 1920; $350. *Courtesy of Steve Johns.*

Here is the reverse side of the McCandless Mazda Lamp sign.

Few logos are as appealing to collectors as Conoco's Minuteman. This rare 16" diameter flanged version has what it takes to score big with collectors; c. 1920s, Rare. *Courtesy of Rick Trotnic.*

The graphics do the talking on this Goodyear flanged sign; c. 1920, 20" x 32", $850. *Courtesy of Tom and Sherry Watt.*

17

Gulf Gasoline used this familiar logo for many years, here on a flanged sign; c. 1930s, 25" x 20", $650. *Courtesy of Tom and Sherry Watt*

Red Hat used this round motor oil-gasoline sign in the 1920s; 30", $3,000. *Courtesy of Dave and Kathy Lane.*

Standard Oil Company of Nebraska used this flanged, two-sided Polarine Motor Oils sign in the 1920s; 22" x 18", $500. *Courtesy of John Bobroff*

Pure Oil and High Speed were independent companies until they merged in the 1930s. Here is a flanged sign which advertises early credit cards; $400. *Courtesy of Rod Krupka.*

These two rest room signs are from the Whilshire Oil Company in Louisiana and date from the 1950s. Signs that might have appeared run-of-the-mill were given considerable improvement with the addition of the two silhouettes; $500/pair. *Courtesy of John Bobroff.*

General Gasoline used this two-sided, round lubester sign in the 1920s; 8", $650. *Courtesy of John Romagnoli.*

Mobil produced a variety of shield-shaped pump signs featuring their famous Pegasus logo through the years. Many designs were made in the thousands. However, this Mobilheat sign complete with lower marquee is certainly the exception; $600. *Private collection.*

"Veedol: 100% Pennsylvania." Plain and simple, flat and one-sided, it dates from the 1930s; 42" x 14", $400. *Courtesy of Mick Hoover.*

Standard Oil Company gets the message across with this king-size, two-sided, flanged Crown Gasoline sign. It dates from the 1920s and features their well-known crown trademark; $800. *Courtesy of Mick Hoover.*

This flanged two-sided Polarine sign dates from the 1920s and incorporates their Stanocola logo at the bottom right; $1,500. *Courtesy of John Romagnoli.*

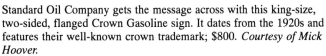

Shell Petroleum used this die-cut Shell Kerosene sign around 1930; $1,000. *Courtesy of Tom Licouris.*

This die-cut Aristo Motor Oil sign features their logo on a shield-shaped, flanged sign; c. 1920s, $1,700. *Courtesy of Wendall White.*

This small sized, flanged, two-sided Harris Oils sign is popular with collectors. Its oil barrel graphics give it plenty of eye-appeal; 21" x 17", $2500. *Courtesy of John Romagnoli.*

Many petroleum companies made a special effort to promote the advantages of a clean engine. Standard Oil Company of California followed through with this unusual-shaped flanged Crankcase Cleaning Service sign. The use of the Calol and Zerolene logos score big with collectors; c. 1925, $2,000. *Courtesy of Tom Licouris.*

Pendol Motor Oil produced this small, flanged sign in the era around 1920. The outstanding graphics at the top make this one a keeper. Notice the slogan. Approximately 13" x 17", $1,000. *Courtesy of Tom Licouris.*

Here's a closeup of the beautiful logos found on the Crankcase Cleaning Service sign. It is interesting to note that both logos incorporate a bear in their graphics.

This die-cut Goodyear Motorcycle sign's outstanding graphics have appeal to non-petro enthusiasts as well. It is flanged and two-sided; c. 1930, approximately 28" x 20", $5000. *Courtesy of Tom Licouris.*

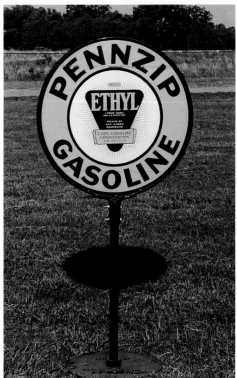
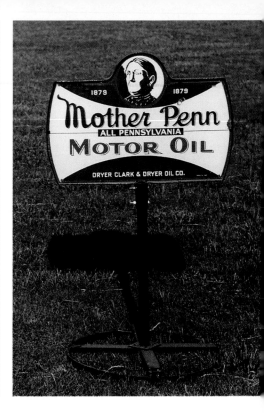

The four lollipop signs depicted here are typical of the dozens manufactured through the years. Each is flat, two-sided, and comes complete with stand and metal base. Notice that the Penn-Drake Motor Oil sign has an embossed base. This adds considerably to the sign's desirability. These were mostly manufactured in the 1920s-'40s. Conoco, $650; Pennzip, $600; Mother Penn, $800, and Penn-Drake, $2,000. *Courtesy of Bill and Karen Brown and Dave and Kathy Lane.*

This Kendall Motor Oils sign was hung from a bracket; c. 1930, 24" x 18", $300. *Courtesy of John Bobroff.*

This Johnson Gasoline Ethyl sign was distributed by Burdick in Chicago. It features their famous winged "Time Tells" logo; c. 1920, 24", $3,000. *Courtesy of Dave and Kathy Lane.*

Although the manufacturer of this Texaco 2 Quart Motor Oil sign is unknown, you can be sure that the intricate graphics and color scheme used were somewhat of a nightmare in the manufacturing process; approximately 16" x 18", $1500. *Courtesy of Tom Licouris.*

St. Helens Gasoline was a southern California company controlled by British investors; c. 1930s. 30", $600. *Courtesy of John Bobroff.*

Gene's Shell was an independent distributor that went to the expense of having their own custom-made porcelain signs; approximately 30", $2,500. *Courtesy of Tom Licouris.*

Pierce Oil Corporation used this convex Pennant Oils sign in the era around 1915; approximately 16", $800. *Courtesy of Tom Licouris.*

23

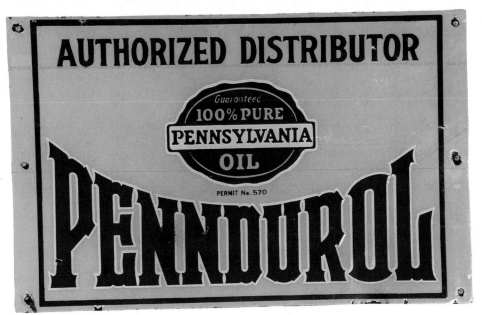

Penndurol put this "Authorized Distributor" sign in service during the 1930s, featuring the Pennsylvania Oil logo; 24" x 15", $300. *Courtesy of John Bobroff.*

Sierra Gasoline was marketed in the early years in California. Although the sign pictured here is somewhat in the rough, its rarity and outstanding graphics more than make up for condition; c. 1930, 30", $2,000. *Courtesy of John Bobroff.*

The seaplane featured at the top of this Harbor Petroleum Products sign rates high with collectors; c. 1940s, $4,000. *Courtesy of Tom Licouris.*

If pump plates are your thing, this rare Hancock Gasoline model should fit in your collection nicely. Their well-known bird with cane makes a graphic statement; c. 1940s, approximately 12", $900. *Courtesy of John Romagnoli.*

This Koolmotor Oil sign was designed to be used in a sidewalk lollipop stand. Its unusual shape and beautiful graphics make it a standout; $1,700. *Courtesy of Tom Licouris.*

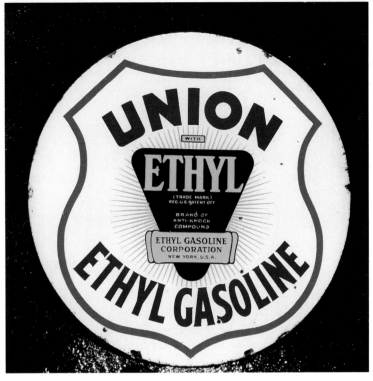

Union Ethyl Gasoline utilizes their shield logo in red outline on this two-sided sign; c. 1930s, 30", $600. *Courtesy of John Bobroff.*

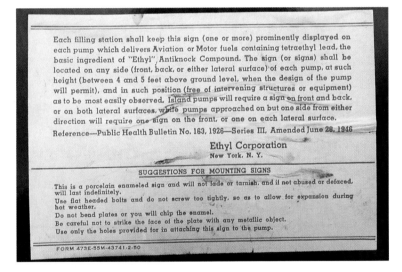

The "Contains Lead motor fuel sign shown here was manufactured by the tens of thousands. Maybe in the millions. Who knows? Most states had laws which required that this sign be prominently placed on each pump. Many pumps had two. Although the lead motor fuel sign is of minimal interest, the decal shown here was affixed to the reverse and shows the exact position of the Ethyl Corporation regarding sign placement; $10. *Courtesy of Rod Krupka.*

Continental Oil Company must have figured this rest room sign would increase sales. This unusual piece is ink-stamped at lower right, "Property of Continental Oil Company;" c. 1930, 10" x 10", $250. *Courtesy of Mick Hoover.*

25

This Iso-Vis Motor Oil sign was designed to be used on a lubester; c. 1920. 7", $600. *Courtesy of Dave and Kathy Lane.*

This die-cut Packard Service sign takes on the distinctive shape of an early front-end radiator. Although it may seem inconsequential, the attached radiator cap at top is often missing from similar signs; $1,800. *Courtesy of Tom and Susan Dahl.*

Sunray's attractive eight-sided logo found its place on this small sign. It was no doubt used in bulk station operations, although many other possibilities exist as well; 12" x 9", $350. *Courtesy of Randy Reith.*

What appears to be two separate signs in the photograph is actually a rare Shell Ethyl combination sign. The Ethyl sign is part of the Shell sign and dates from the early years of Ethyl additives in the 1930s; $1,300. *Courtesy of Tom and Susan Dahl.*

One of the most attractive Texaco signs is this "Marine Lubricants" example. It was used primarily at marinas; c. 1940, $1,300. *Courtesy of Dave and Kathy Lane.*

This flat one-sided Fletcher Oil sign dates from the 1930s; 16",
$1,250. *Courtesy of John Romagnoli.*

Most service stations offered free air to motorists in need. However,
few Shell Petroleum Stations used this die-cut sign; approximately
14" x 14", $900. *Courtesy of Tom and Susan Dahl.*

Richlube Motor Oil is advertised on this
two-sided sign from the 1930s; 24"; $2,500.
Courtesy of Tom Licouris.

Fort Pitt Motor Oil is found on this two-sided sign designed to hang
from a bracket; c. 1930s; 22" x 28", $750. *Courtesy of Tom
Licouris.*

The beautiful monoplane and race car
graphics add considerably to the desirability
of this Ace High two-sided sign; c. 1930s,
23" x 17", $3,000. *Courtesy of Tom
Licouris.*

Associated Gasoline used this eye-catching sign with a one-gallon container in the 1930s; 23.5", $1,200. *Courtesy of Tom Licouris.*

This striking Nash Authorized Service sign is shown complete with its original bracket. Its interesting combination of eye-catching graphics combined with Nash advertising gives the necessary eye appeal; c. 1930, approximately 24" x 40", $2,300. *Courtesy of Jerry and Phyllis Miller.*

This Globe Battery Station sign is flat and two sided; c. 1940s, 20", $600. *Courtesy of Tom Licouris.*

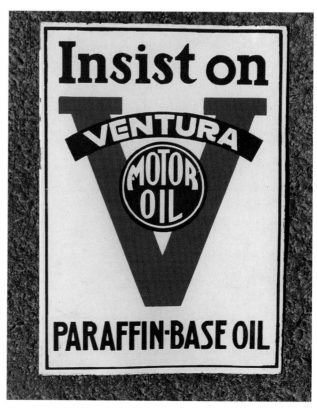

The 1920s saw the use of this Ventura Motor Oil sign; 13" x 18", $650. *Courtesy of John Romagnoli.*

Oak Motor Oil is featured on this sign, which was designed to be hung from a bracket; approximately 28" x 17", $1,400. *Author's Collection.*

The Independent Oilmen's Association logo was placed prominently on this sign; 32", $1,500. *Courtesy of Dave and Kathy Lane.*

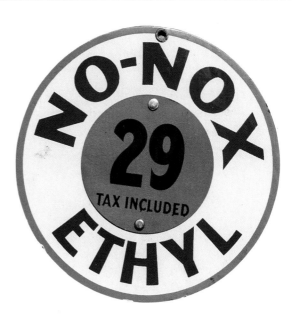

No-Nox Ethyl was a product of the Gulf Oil Company. This round No-Nox sign was placed on their pumps and featured a special insert that could be removed if the price per gallon changed. Although the base sign is porcelain, the removable pricing insert was baked enamel; $200. *Courtesy of Rod Krupka.*

This Texaco Crankcase Service sign dates from the 1920s. Notice that the word "Golden" was given a separate color with a black outline on the lettering. This brings the total colors on this sign up to six; 28" x 22", $750. *Courtesy of John Romagnoli.*

Pacific Tires gave you a visual image of their product on this big sign; c. 1940s, 48" x 22", $250. *Private Collection.*

Hamman Gasoline is seen on this pump plate dating from the 1940s; 10" x 10", $350. *Courtesy of John Romagnoli.*

This unusual one-sided Union Oil Company No Smoking sign dates from the 1930s; 19" x 19", $500. *Courtesy of Tom Licouris.*

Shellubrication used this two-sided octagon sign in the 1930s; $600. *Courtesy of Mick Hoover.*

Zerolene Motor Oil is featured on this two-sided sign dating from the 1920s; 27" x 27", $900. *Courtesy of Mick Hoover.*

"Satisfies from Pole to Pole" was the slogan used by Manhattan Oil Company for their Trop-Artic brand motor oil; 30", $2,500. *Courtesy of Dave and Kathy Lane.*

Quaker State Cold Test Oil is featured on this strip sign. The two-sided sign was designed to be hung from a bracket. The fine print ink-stamped at bottom left reads "property of Q.S. Oil Refinery, Baltimore Enamel, 200 Fifth Avenue, New York;" c. 1930s, 26.5" x 6", $350. *Courtesy of Mick Hoover.*

This beautiful Wings Regular Gasoline pump plate dates from the 1950s; $1,500. *Courtesy of Rick Trotnic.*

Utoco stood for Utah Oil Company and was a subsidiary of Standard Oil. The sign features raised embossing on a familiar Standard Oil die-cut background; c. 1940. 14.5" x 13", $500. *Courtesy of Tom Licouris.*

Polarine used this two-sided sign in the 1920s. At the bottom is ink-stamped "Burdick Consumers Building, Chicago and Balto Enamel and Novelty Co. MD;" 28", $500. *Courtesy of Mick Hoover.*

Willard was a best-selling American battery for years. This Willard Service Station example dates to the era around 1920 and was meant to hang on a bracket. The fine print at the bottom left reads "Copyright by the Willard Storage Battery Company, October 1917;" 30" x 14", $400. *Courtesy of Mick Hoover.*

An eagle in flight sets the theme on this Gasco Motor Fuel sign from the 1930s; $2,000. *Courtesy of Tom Licouris.*

Magnolia Gasoline was a product of the Standard Oil Company of New York. This sign was manufactured by Veribrite of Chicago, Illinois; 30", $1,200. *Courtesy of Dave and Kathy Lane.*

This unusual No Smoking sign was manufactured by Veribrite Signs in the 1930s. It is ink-stamped at the bottom right; 19" x 4", $350. *Courtesy of Tom Licouris.*

The General Petroleum Corporation of California issued this certification sign to those dealers offering lubrication services. Notice the unusual ribbon at the bottom left which shows the Pegasus and Gargoyle logos together; c. 1935, 16" x 19", $1,200. *Courtesy of Tom Licouris.*

Bay Regular Gasoline used this die-cut sign in the 1940s; 10.5" x 12", $600. *Courtesy of Tom Licouris.*

This Gilmore No Smoking strip sign is rare and dates to around 1930; 36" x 6", $3,000. *Courtesy of Tom Licouris.*

One of the most beautiful logos used on petroleum products is Standard Oil Company's Stanocola insignia; 30", $2,500. *Courtesy of Dave and Kathy Lane.*

The Ethyl Gasoline logo was placed prominently on this Globe Petroleum sign. Notice the various forms of transportation which encircle the sign; 30", $1,200. *Courtesy of Dave and Kathy Lane.*

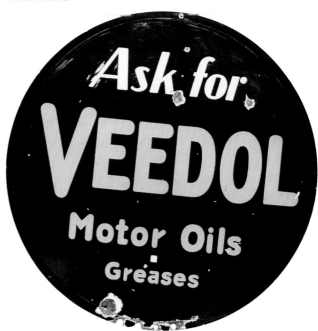

This Veedol sign dates from the 1930s; 23.5", $350. *Courtesy of Mick Hoover.*

This beautiful Royaline Gasoline sign dates to the 1920s; 30", $2,200. *Courtesy of Dave and Kathy Lane.*

This small Mother Penn Motor Oil lubester sign dates to around 1930; $700. *Courtesy of Dave and Kathy Lane.*

This Kendall Motor Oil is unusual in the respect that the colors have been reversed from those normally encountered; c. 1930s, 23.5", $400. *Courtesy of Mick Hoover.*

Yellow Knight's outstanding logo is the centerpiece of this sign; c. 1930, 30", $2,200. *Courtesy of Dave and Kathy Lane.*

This small King Gasoline sign was no doubt used on a visible pump as evidenced by the telltale mounting holes at right; c. 1925, 12", $1,200. *Courtesy of Tom Licouris.*

This Union Oil Company shield sign dates from the 1930s; 7" x 7", $1,000. *Courtesy of Tom Licouris.*

It seems the variety of No Smoking signs goes on and on. This rare Sunset Products strip sign dates to about 1930; 30" x 6", $1,500. *Courtesy of Tom Licouris.*

The base for this Paraland Motor Oil lollipop sign seems to have grown legs. Fortunately the best part was left behind for others to enjoy; $1,800. *Courtesy of John Alinder.*

Standard Heating Oils used this unusual pump sign in the 1950s, incorporating a three-colored chevron; 10" x 12.5", $375. *Courtesy of Steve Parker.*

Although this Pennzoil Lubrication sign may appear to date from the 1950s, it actually was manufactured around 1930; 27" x 15", $300. *Courtesy of John Bobroff.*

Conoco wanted to make sure that motorists knew their gasoline products contained Ethyl; c. 1930, 26", $1,500. *Courtesy of Dave and Kathy Lane.*

The military uniform found on this Pan-Am Motor Oil sign would help even a novice date this sign to around 1925. Ink-stamping on the bottom red border reads "ADV. D.S. Reliance ADV. CO;" 30", $2,000. *Courtesy of Dave and Kathy Lane.*

The 1920s saw the use of this Veedol Oil Film Protection sign. It's flanged and two-sided; approximately 22" x 12", $800. *Courtesy of Dave and Kathy Lane.*

The familiar logo of Shell Motor Oil is found on this sign, marked at the bottom left, "Prop. Shell Petroleum Co." and at the bottom right, "Tenn, Enamel Mfg. Co. Nashville, March 1931;" 24", $800. *Courtesy of Dave and Kathy Lane.*

The logo used by Chrysler Plymouth on this two-sided hanging sign is apropos; c. 1930, 22" x 18", $900. *Courtesy of John Bobroff.*

Horsepower Plus was graphically illustrated on this Cosden Liquid Gas Special sign. Ink-stamped at the bottom is "Reliance Adv. Co. Milwaukee;" c. late 1920s, 30", $2,000. *Courtesy of Dave and Kathy Lane.*

Here's another example of how graphics can make a favorable impression on motorists. Texas Pacific utilized an Indian tepee on this street sign. It was manufactured by Veribrite Signs in the late 1920s; 42", $2,500. *Courtesy of Dave and Kathy Lane.*

37

This Icy-Flo Motor Oil sign saw use in a sidewalk lollipop stand; c. 1930s. 24", $550. *Courtesy of Gene and Red Sonnen.*

Harris Oils used this beautiful flanged sign in the 1920s; 22" x 26", $850. *Courtesy of Bill and Karen Brown.*

Johnson Oils used this rare winged sign in the era around 1925. The fine print at the bottom reads, "Burdick Consolidated Consumers Building, Chicago;" 24", $3,000. *Courtesy of Dave and Kathy Lane.*

The 1920s found this round Magnolia Petroleum Company sign in service; 30", $600. *Courtesy of Bill and Karen Brown.*

This rare Saxon Motor Cars sign was manufactured prior to 1925. As unusual as the sign is, possibly its most interesting feature is its obscure manufacturer. At bottom right is ink-stamped, "Ohio Valley Enameling Company, Covington, West Virginia;" 18" x 18", $1,200. *Courtesy of Bill and Karen Brown.*

Conoco Gasoline was manufactured by Continental Oil Company. The example shown here is die-cut not only around its perimeter, but also on the inside; 26" x 26", $700. *Courtesy of Bill and Karen Brown.*

This Ford Genuine Parts V-8 sign looks as American as apple pie. However, this particular sign has its origins in Canada; c. 1934, 29" x 30", $2,700. *Courtesy of Gene and Red Sonnen.*

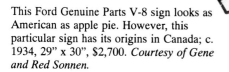

Universal Batteries is the topic of this die-cut, heart-shaped sign dating from the 1930s; 20", $550. *Courtesy of Bill and Karen Brown.*

Gold Medal Oils was marketed by Kunz Petroleum out of the Minneapolis, Minnesota, area beginning in the 1920s. This Gold Medal Oil sign appears to be a candidate for a sidewalk lollipop-type stand. Kunz Petroleum's gasoline products were discontinued in the 1970s. However, Kunz is still in business today as an auto parts supplier; 30", $5,000. *Courtesy of Gene and Red Sonnen.*

Ethyl Gasoline Corporation was featured on this Phillips 66 orange die-cut, two-sided shield; c. 1930s, $550. *Courtesy of Bill and Karen Brown.*

Pure Oil Company produced this trio of 15" diameter signs in the 1930s and '40s. Each sign was destined to be used on a pump certifying a particular grade of fuel; $700 each. *Courtesy of Bill and Karen Brown.*

An oil derrick was the central image of this Gold Star sign; c. 1930, 30", $1,700. *Courtesy of Gene and Red Sonnen.*

Skelly Petroleum produced this Aromax Ethyl sign in the 1930s. It was used in a lollipop stand; 30", $4,800. *Courtesy of Bill and Karen Brown.*

"From Tank Car to Car Tank" was the flashy slogan used by Dixie Vim on this diagonal sign. The tank car and early roadster graphics date this sign to the 1920s; 30" x 30", $2,500. *Courtesy of Gene and Red Sonnen.*

This unusual Red Crown Gasoline sign features the familiar Standard Oil crown trademark superimposed over an unusual Ethyl logo. Notice that in place of the usual Ethyl Gasoline Corporation banner at bottom are the words, "General Motors Product." The ink stamping at the bottom reads "Burdick Consumers Building, Chicago, USA;" c. 1920, 30", $1,500. *Courtesy of Dave and Kathy Lane.*

Bell Oil Company of St. Louis, Missouri, used this strip sign in the 1920s. Notice that they not only produced automobile oil, but also were in the business of manufacturing lamp oils as well; 5" x 30", $1,200. *Courtesy Tom and Susan Dahl.*

Rare would be an appropriate word to describe this Fyre Drop Gasoline pump plate. It has a super-thick coating of porcelain as evidenced by the photograph; c. 1920, 10", $1,000. *Courtesy of Tom and Susan Dahl.*

Phillips Petroleum was the featured brand on this 1930 motor oil sign; approximately 22" x 10", $1,100. *Courtesy of Tom and Susan Dahl.*

It seems as though even small-time manufacturers were trying to use catchy slogans to help sell their products. This Autoline Oil sign gets into the act with its "For your motor's sake" slogan; 30" x 20", $500. *Courtesy of Bill and Karen Brown.*

Kanotex was the abbreviation for Kansas, Oklahoma, and Texas. This sign was designed for a sidewalk lollipop stand; c. 1920s, 30", $600. *Courtesy of Bill and Karen Brown.*

Phillips Petroleum used these signs for their lollipop stands. This particular example has the Ethyl logo superimposed over their familiar 66 shield; 30", $1,500. *Courtesy of Bill and Karen Brown.*

Just when you thought you'd seen it all, something like this Bear Springs sign shows up. Although this particular sign is of Canadian origin (specifically London, Ontario), the bears are an American icon named "Happy Bear" by the Bear Wheel Alignment Company in the United States. Possibly the most unusual feature of this sign is that the bears are red in color. It's flat, two-sided, and designed to be hung from a bracket; approximately 28" x 20", $1,500. *Courtesy of Tom and Susan Dahl.*

Kendall's Pennzbest Motor Oils were advertised on this round lollipop stand sign in the 1930s; 24", $300. *Courtesy of Gene and Red Sonnen.*

Deep-Rock Gasoline and Motor Oils used this two-sided sign around 1930; 30" x 24", $350. *Courtesy of Gene and Red Sonnen.*

Many of the best porcelain signs ever manufactured were designed to be used in conjunction with neon lettering. This Buick "Valve in Head" example dates from the 1930s; 42", $1,500. *Courtesy of Dave and Kathy Lane.*

Here's another example of the endless stream of sidewalk lollipop stand signs. This one was produced for Sinclair. Notice the early Sinclair dinosaur, which is featured on their earliest signs dating prior to 1930; 24", $2,500. *Courtesy of Dave and Kathy Lane.*

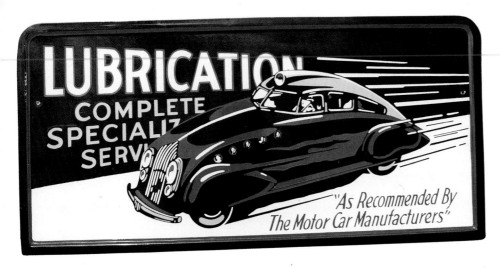

Outstanding graphics are featured on this Complete Specialized Lubrication sign. It is flat and one-sided, with a self-framed perimeter. The unusual looking car may stump even the best antique auto enthusiast as it is actually a conglomeration of styles from many motor cars of the day. The sign itself is also quite generic as it could have been used by any lubrication shop; 42" x 20", $6,000. *Courtesy of Gene and Red Sonnen.*

This super Nourse Motor Oil lubester sign dates from the 1920s; $2,000. *Courtesy of Dave and Kathy Lane.*

Rest room signs have become popular among petro sign collectors. These two small-sized signs are from the 1940s and were used on Sunoco Station rest rooms; $250 each. *Courtesy of Tom and Susan Dahl.*

Hood Tires used this rectangular sign in the era around 1925. It's designed to be hung from a bracket; $2,000. *Courtesy of Tom and Susan Dahl.*

This unidentified No Smoking sign is actually intended to be used at Sinclair Stations as evidenced by its telltale green and red lettering on white background; approximately 20" x 18", $400. *Courtesy of W.K. Richards.*

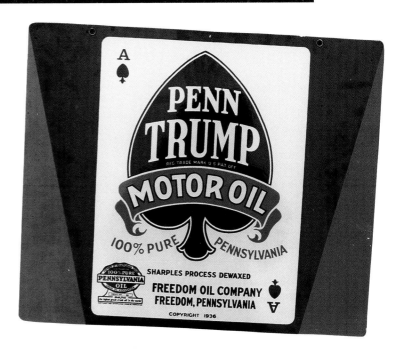

This two-sided Colonial Lubrication Service sign was used in the 1940s; 30" x 30", $600. *Courtesy of Gene and Red Sonnen.*

This beautiful Penn Trump Motor Oil sign is two sided and was designed to be hung from a bracket; c. 1935, $2,000. *Courtesy of Tom and Susan Dahl.*

USL Batteries are featured on this self-framed sign dating from the 1930s; 60" x 17.5", $350. *Courtesy of Gene and Red Sonnen.*

Nitro-Valspar was an automotive finish popular in the 1920s, like the automobile of the day pictured bottom right; 20" x 28", $1,000. *Courtesy of Gene and Red Sonnen.*

This William Penn Motor Oil sign was designed to fit into a sidewalk stand; c. 1930s, $900. *Courtesy of Tom and Susan Dahl.*

Graphics abound on this two-sided Economy Auto sign; c. 1940, 18" x 36.5", $2,800. *Courtesy of Gene and Red Sonnen.*

Chapter Two

Flat One- & Two-Sided Signs

The signs in this chapter were manufactured with the advertising either on one or both sides. You will notice that the placement of the mounting holes changes from one sign to the next. Each design called for a different support method. Many of the signs in this chapter were designed to be hung from a metal bracket. Others were designed to be mounted on a wall. Still others could be found fastened to a cart or a cooler. A few wound up on the sides of trucks. Occasionally, signs are found fastened to one another, identical copies mounted back-to-back.

One of America's most recognizable figures is that of Elsie the cow seen on this die-cut Borden's Ice Cream sign; c. 1940s, 38" x 40", $2,500. *Courtesy of Chuck Witte.*

This flanged Ingersoll Watches sign dates to somewhere around 1930 and takes on the shape of their then-familiar pocket watch; c. 1930, 8" x 12", $950. *Courtesy of John Romagnoli.*

The bus on the front of this Pacific Lines Greyhound Depot sign dates to the late 1930s. This die-cut beauty was designed to be hung from a steel bracket; 36" x 24", $2500. *Courtesy of Tom Licouris.*

In the 1930s, many farms were plagued by chicken thieves. This sign told potential poultry pluckers to shop elsewhere; 14" x 13", $600. *Author's Collection.*

Ton-Gors produced this four-color, die-cut sign in the 1930s; approximately 32" x 38", $900. *Author's Collection.*

United States Express Company used this winged box superimposed over a horseshoe as their logo. The ink stamping at bottom right of this early beauty reads "Brilliant Mfg. Co. Phila. PA;" c. 1895, 20" x 12", $1,500. *Courtesy of Bill and Belinda Fraser.*

This Metzger's Milk sign dates from the 1930s and takes on the familiar shape of a milk bottle from that era; $1,700. *Courtesy of Dave and Kathy Lane.*

This Drink Dr. Pepper sign is self-framed, with its red center image offset by a green border; c. 1940, 26" x 12", $450. *Courtesy of Randy Reith.*

Piedmont was a familiar brand of cigarettes during the 1930s; approximately 16" x 7", $350. *Courtesy of Randy Reith.*

The wonderful graphics on this Camel Cigarette sign give the necessary visual impact; c. 1940, approximately 26" x 11", $550. *Courtesy of Randy Reith.*

The beautiful graphics found on this Recruit Little Cigars sign make this piece very desirable; c. 1915, 30" x 12", $1,200. *Courtesy of Pete Keim.*

United States Express used this "Money Orders Sold Here sign, manufactured by Ingram-Richardson sometime around 1915; 24" x 12", $1,500. *Courtesy of Bill and Belinda Fraser.*

Hamm's Beer of St. Paul, Minnesota, produced this outstanding sign sometime around 1895. The fantastic central image of this piece was done with a lithographic process detailed in the accompanying photograph; 14", $750. *Courtesy of Pete Keim.*

Here's a close-up of the monumental graphic work featured on the Hamm's sign. Every small detail in the eagle can be seen clearly. The wingtips were designed to protrude through the central image area to help give perspective and dimension to the graphics. This piece is truly a work of art! *Courtesy of Pete Keim.*

Southern Express Company produced this Money Orders sign in the late 1800s. The ink stamping at bottom left reads, "Made In England," which was typical of those early pieces still being produced for American companies by English manufacturers before the turn of the century; 12" x 10", $1,800. *Courtesy of Bill and Belinda Fraser.*

This beautiful, slightly curved Canadian Pacific die-cut sign was designed to be used on the front end of early diesel locomotives in the 1940s and '50s; 24" x 38", $1,200. *Courtesy of John Bobroff.*

WOOL SOAP

The era around 1910 found this Wool Soap strip sign in service; 24" x 3.5", $600. *Courtesy of John Bobroff.*

Despite a little edge roughness, the graphics on this Old Coon Cigars sign still make this an oldie but goodie; c. 1910, 15" x 15", $400. *Courtesy of John Bobroff.*

Gerber and Bear was an alarm company manufacturer located in southern California. This one-sided sign fastened to the front of one of their alarms; c. 1950, 9" x 9", $100. *Courtesy of John Bobroff.*

GMAC was in the credit business as far back as the 1930s. This Cards Honored Here sign dates from that era; 24" x 12", $600. *Courtesy of John Romagnoli.*

Many small town merchants wanted the public to know that the store they were shopping in was locally owned and operated. Notice that there was a flower pattern placed around each of the grommets in this "Home Owned Store" sign; c. 1930s, approximately 18" x 12", $450. *Courtesy of Frank Feher.*

51

This Castle Gate Coal sign is one of three rectangular signs made to advertise their products in the 1930s and 40s. Castle Gate Coal was owned by the Denver and Rio Grande Western Railway. Their production facility was located in Utah and the graphics on this sign feature the rock formations of Castle Gate, Utah, a well-known landmark; 30" x 12", $500. *Courtesy of John Bobroff.*

The Big Four Route was the Cleveland, Cincinnati, Chicago, and St. Louis Railway. This Cross Tracks in Second Gear sign was produced for them sometime in the 1920s; 24" x 18", $500. *Courtesy of John Bobroff.*

This Loth's Stoves & Ranges sign was manufactured by Baltimore Enamel & Novelty company as seen by the ink stamping at the bottom. The beautiful scrolled work and serifed graphics were typical of those used in the years of early porcelain enamel advertising; c. 1900, 14" x 20", $750. *Courtesy of John Bobroff.*

Southern Pacific Lines produced this Pick-Up and Delivery Service sign for the sides of their trucks; c. 1930s, 21" x 16", $800. *Courtesy of John Bobroff.*

Who says cement signs have to be boring? Lawrence Portland Cement Company of Siegfried, Pennsylvania, used this beauty around 1920; 16" x 16", $300. *Courtesy of Jeffery Ingram Sherill.*

Bewley's Anchor Feeds has "Veribrite Signs of Chicago" ink stamped on its reverse side; c. 1940s, 16" x 25", $300. *Courtesy of John Bobroff.*

This die-cut Triple K Service sign takes on the familiar shape of a cup and saucer; c. 1930s, 24" x 18", $350. *Courtesy of John Romagnoli.*

Chicago Aurora and Elgin Railroad placed this sign near their railroad stations; c. 1930, 34" x 34", $1,000. *Courtesy of John Bobroff.*

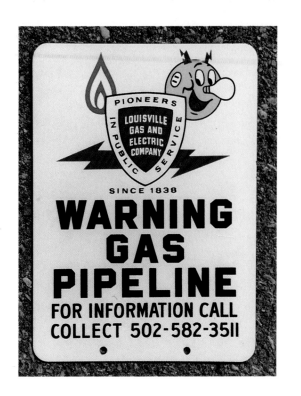

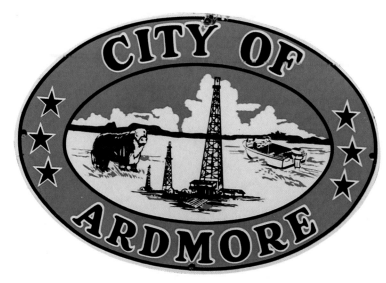

This oval City of Ardmore sign was made in the 1950s; 16" x 12", $250. *Courtesy of Wendall White.*

The very collectible Reddy Kilowatt shows his face on this Louisville Gas and Electric Company Pipeline sign; c. 1950s, approximately 10" x 14", $300. *Courtesy of Wendall White.*

Mazzio's Pizza used this two-piece porcelain advertisement in the 1950s, possibly on the sides of trucks; $200. *Courtesy of Wendall White.*

The State of Colorado had this Park & Recreation Board sign manufactured in 1961 as seen by the accompanying photograph. Quite possibly this was the only one ever produced, as this sample is the only one known; $250. *Courtesy of Wendall White.*

Here's a view of the reverse side of the Colorado Park & Recreation Board sign. It was typical to inscribe the date on samples just as was done here. *Courtesy of Wendall White.*

Tuberculosis was an ever-present threat in the early part of this century. The sign presented here is a reminder of this pervasive problem in America. The sign was supported with the help of the bracket on the right; approximately 11" x 15" including the ornamental scrollwork at top, $450. *Courtesy of Layne Christensen.*

Carnation produced a fair amount of these die-cut Ice Cream signs in the 1940s and '50s. However, trying to locate one may be a difficult task as collectors have eagerly sought them out; $800. *Courtesy of Layne Christensen.*

Speed Queen Washers and Ironers advertised on this two-sided sign; c. 1940s, 24" x 10", $200. *Courtesy of Lee and Bonnie Kollorz.*

This is a scarce American Railway Express sign; c. 1920s, 11" x 11", $450. *Courtesy of Lee and Bonnie Kollorz.*

The Iron Fireman manufactured self-stoking coal burners for home heating; c. 1930s, 12", $250. *Courtesy of Lee and Bonnie Kollorz.*

Rochester, New York, was home to the W.H. Clark Company, which produced this Canned Foods sign in the 1920s; approximately 17" x 21", $750. *Author's Collection.*

The Farm Bureau Association gave a graphic representation of what they were all about on this beautiful sign; c. 1940s, 16", $650. *Courtesy of Dave and Kathy Lane.*

This die-cut running Reddy Kilowatt figure may appear to be flat. However, it is actually two inches thick, and hollow in the center; c. 1950s, 30" x 40", $1,000. *Courtesy of Bill and Karen Brown.*

Philgas Service sent out a simple message; c. 1930s, 14" x 6", $325. *Courtesy of Bill and Karen Brown.*

It's hard to beat the exceptional graphics found on this Good Humor Ice Cream sign from the 1950s. Similar signs can still be found in service on Good Humor trucks today; $800. *Courtesy of Layne Christensen.*

Red Man Scrap Tobacco is featured on this one-sided sign; c. 1930s, 16", $375. *Courtesy of Bill and Belinda Fraser.*

Ingram Richardson manufactured this King & Co. Draymen Warehousemen sign; c. 1920s, $250. *Courtesy of Jeffery Ingram Sherill.*

This flat sign was designed to be hung from a bracket. It was manufactured by Orme Evans & Company Ltd., West Hampton; 30" x 20", $500. *Courtesy of Bill and Belinda Fraser.*

This two-sided Ben-Hur Grocer sign is marked "property of Coffee Products of America Incorporated Limited;" c. 1930s, 18" x 24", $2,700. *Courtesy of John Romagnoli.*

The word "Protection" is actually written onto a roof above this beautiful Rexall Store sign, offering the viewer a three-dimensional representation; c. 1930, approximately 28" x 40" without the bracket, $2,500. *Courtesy of Jim Oswald.*

This Pensupreme Ice Cream sign was designed to be used in a sidewalk stand; c. 1940 era, $1,100. *Courtesy of Jim Oswald.*

Purity Ice Cream is featured on this die-cut sign; c. 1935, 20" x 12", $800. *Courtesy of Michael Villamagna.*

This Liberty Coal sign is a standout. The beautiful graphics leave an impression which is not easily forgotten; c. 1930s, 13" x 18", $1,000. *Courtesy of Jim Oswald.*

Coca-Cola had these large size signs placed prominently in the 1930s on many establishments throughout America. The word "billiards" at the top was actually hand painted over the word "confectionery" which was part of the original sign. Most of these signs were manufactured by Tennessee Enamel; $2,250. *Courtesy of Jim Oswald.*

Pabst Wonder Cheese produced this sign in the era around 1935; $1,200. *Courtesy of Jim Oswald.*

Collectors with good taste will appreciate this San Felice Cigars sign from the 1930s; 39" x 13", $300. *Courtesy of Michael Villamagna.*

7-Up was all that was needed to get the message across on this flat one-sided sign dating from the 1950s; $250. *Courtesy of Jeffery Ingram Sherill.*

S & H Green Stamps were a popular giveaway for years. This display sign dates from 1956 and is flat and two-sided; $200. *Courtesy of Jeffery Ingram Sherill.*

This small, no trespassing sign dates from the 1930s; $175. *Courtesy of Jeffery Ingram Sherill.*

This small "Stop Accidents" sign was manufactured for company trucks belonging to Bell System Subsidiaries; c. 1920s, 3", $300. *Author's Collection.*

This sign was used on bulldozers like the one illustrated. Shaw Sales & Service was a local Allis Chalmers dealership located in Los Angeles; c. 1940s, $150. *Courtesy of John Romagnoli.*

Although its exact use is uncertain, this sign was quite likely placed on company trucks; c. 1930s, 6", $350. *Courtesy of John Romagnoli.*

National Express Company had this sign in service around the turn of the century; 18" x 16", $1,500. *Courtesy of Bill and Belinda Fraser.*

Kleinheinz Ice Cream is seen on this two-sided sidewalk sign; c 1940s, $400. *Courtesy of Parkside Antique Mall.*

Pepsi-Cola used this unusual guitar-pick-shaped sign in the 1940s; approximately 36" x 40", $450. *Courtesy of George Jacques.*

Beautiful graphics abound on this flanged Breinigs Lithogen Paint sign; c. 1920s, approximately 14" x 22", $850. *Courtesy of John Rutske.*

This decal has seen better days. It was photographed in its natural state, on the back of an early sign. Although it's hard to make out, notice that Baltimore Enamel & Novelty Company put the manager's name on their decal. *Courtesy of John Bobroff.*

Baltimore Enamel & Novelty manufactured this Orange County Ice Cream sign around 1930; 18" x 24", $350. *Courtesy of John Bobroff.*

For years, signals were an important form of communication in the day-to-day operations of mines. This Arizona State Code of Mine Bell Signals sign lists the official roster of standard communication signals in mines. It was in use as early as 1912, as seen at the lower left; approximately 18" x 40", $700. *Courtesy of Dick Marrah.*

Valley Express Company saw this sign in use during the 1920s; $1,000. *Courtesy of Dick Marrah.*

This small die-cut Schlitz sign was actually part of a larger display; c. 1930s, 15", $400. *Courtesy of Dick Marrah.*

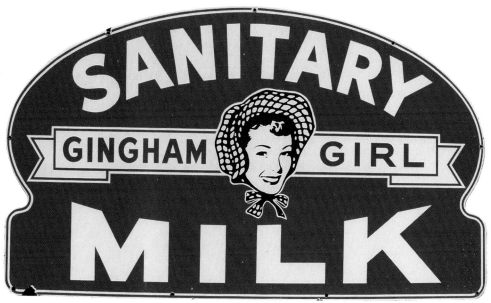

Woodland, California, was home to Gingham Girl Sanitary Milk. The large sign pictured here was no doubt used on company trucks; 41" x 24", $650. *Courtesy of John Bobroff.*

Prairie Farms Butter is a sure bet for collectors of today's country store items. Its outstanding graphics feature a die-cut butter box along with the Illinois Producer Creameries logo, $600. *Courtesy of Dick Marrah.*

M&S Beverages were located in Flint, Michigan; c. 1940s, 30" x 13", $350. *Courtesy of Gene and Red Sonnen.*

Finck's Overalls were a popular brand for years. This flat, one-sided sign has their familiar pig logo at right. $2,000. *Courtesy of Dick Marrah.*

63

F.R. Rice Mercantile Company used this Agent Cigar sign in the 1920s; 28" x 3", $300. *Courtesy of Bill and Belinda Fraser.*

Dr. Scholl's Zino-Pads are graphically represented on this flat, one-sided sign; c. 1930s, $450. *Courtesy of Tom and Susan Dahl.*

Blackstone Cigars are advertised plain and simple on this strip sign. Many of these wound up as kick plates on doors. However, judging by the condition here it must have found service elsewhere; 24" x 3", $150. *Courtesy of Bill and Belinda Fraser.*

Pepsi-Cola used this large, one-sided sign in the 1940s; 40", $650. *Courtesy of Steve Stromski.*

Many of these die-cut Kodak Film signs were made of baked enamel on sheet metal. However, the beauty pictured here is made of porcelain. It was designed to be hung from a bracket and dates from the 1930s; $1,200. *Courtesy of Tom and Susan Dahl.*

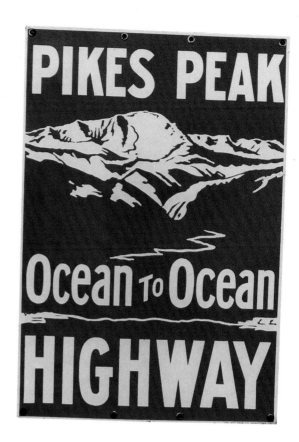

"His Master's Voice" is one of the most recognized trademarks in America. The RCA Corporation had this graphic sign manufactured around 1930. As the story goes, this particular sign was found in a group, not in the United States, but in all places, India; $2,000. *Courtesy of Tom and Susan Dahl.*

This like-new Pikes Peak Ocean to Ocean Highway sign was manufactured by California Metal Enameling Company of Bairdstown, California, and adorned America's byways sometime in the 1930s; 14" x 20", $550. *Courtesy of Gene and Red Sonnen.*

The 1940s saw the use of this Hubbard's Bone Base Fertilizer sign; 22" x 10", $375. *Courtesy of Dick and Kathy Purvis.*

This Kentucky's Best Red Clover Coal sign is flat, one-sided, and dates from the 1940s; $250. *Courtesy of More Antiques.*

One of the most beautiful railway signs ever manufactured has to be this Santa Fe Scout multi-colored sign. The outstanding cowboy graphics coupled with its railway motif appeals to many collectors. These signs are quite rare. This particular one originated from the railroad station in Modesto, California; 40.5" x 20.5", $5,000. *Courtesy of Tom Licouris.*

The die-cut Coca-Cola bottle shown here was actually part of a larger display; c. 1935, 4" x 16", $450. *Courtesy of Tom and Susan Dahl.*

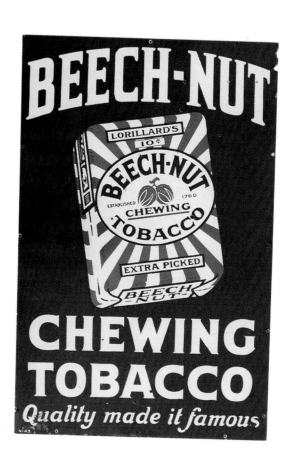

What a piece! High-powered country store graphics abound in this Scratch Feeds sign dating from the 1920s; 27.5" x 19.5", $2,200. *Courtesy of Pete Keim.*

Beech-Nut Chewing Tobacco gets the message across big with this large 24" x 40" sign; c. 1940s, $600. *Courtesy of Kelley Hasselback.*

This unusual sign was used by a livestock equipment supplier for the motion picture industry; c. 1940, 24" x 16", $500. *Courtesy of Tom Licouris.*

This King Arthur Flour sign dates from around 1910. At the bottom is the unusual ink stamping, "Baltimore Enamel & Novelty Company, Baltimore, MD, 103 Eustis Street, Boston;" 18" square, $550. *Courtesy of Pete Keim.*

Inland States used this two-sided depot sign in the 1930s; 24", $2,500. *Courtesy of Tom Licouris.*

The era around 1915 saw this Monkey Brand Polish sign in service; 18" x 9"; $700. *Courtesy of Pete Keim.*

Lithographed graphics make up the central focus of this King's Candies sign; c. 1910, 16" x 20", $1,500. *Courtesy of John Romagnoli.*

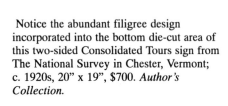

Marin County Milk Company used a Cream Top bottle to advertise their milk products in the 1920s; 6" x 12", $400. *Courtesy of Pete Keim.*

Notice the abundant filigree design incorporated into the bottom die-cut area of this two-sided Consolidated Tours sign from The National Survey in Chester, Vermont; c. 1920s, 20" x 19", $700. *Author's Collection.*

This Colonial Anthracite sign was in service around 1930; 12" x 12", $300. *Courtesy of Dick Marrah.*

Western Express Company used this small Money Orders sign around 1920; 20" x 10", $1,200. *Courtesy of Dick Marrah.*

This Union Ice sign was possibly used on company trucks; c. 1920s, 36", $2,500. *Courtesy of Dick Marrah.*

How's this for eye-catching graphics? This Calaveras Cement Company sign could appeal to almost anyone. The ink stamping at the bottom reads "Baltimore Enamel, 200 Fifth Avenue, New York;" c. 1920, 20" x 20", $950. *Courtesy of John Romagnoli.*

Obak Cigarettes are advertised on this sign; c. 1915, 40" x 10", $600. *Courtesy of John Romagnoli.*

This die-cut Cafe Salada Coffee sign was produced in the 1930s by VEP Limited, Orilla, Ontario; 12" x 13", $350. *Courtesy of John Romagnoli.*

Red Rooster Fruit & Produce used this sign in the 1930s; 20", $1,500. *Courtesy of John Romagnoli.*

There were literally hundreds of beer
manufacturers in the United States
competing for attention in the 1920s.
Weinhard Beer captured the public eye with
its graphic center logo. The ink stamping at
the bottom reads "B.S. Company 166 North
State Street, Chicago and Baltimore Enamel
& Novelty Company MD;" 14" x 19.5",
$600. *Courtesy of Dick Marrah.*

Heileman's Beer sign saw service in the 1950s; 30" x 24", $250.
Courtesy of John Bobroff.

Columbia Records makes a hit with this two-sided record sign,
designed to be hung from a bracket; 30", $1,800. *Author's Collection.*

Even a novice could date this Sun Insurance
sign to the 1920s. The graphic automobile
logo makes its age obvious; 14" x 20",
$1,000. *Courtesy of Dick Marrah.*

This large Drug Store marquee is actually part of a larger two-piece Coca-Cola sign; c. 1940s, $500. *Courtesy of Lee and Bonnie Kollorz.*

There were literally thousands of soda fountains throughout the United States doing a brisk business in the 1950s. This Coca-Cola sign was no doubt used in one of them. Although these signs were produced in great quantities, collector demand has kept them all but non-existent in the public eye; 27 x 30", $2,000. *Courtesy of Dave and Kathy Lane.*

Market Street Railway Company used this unusual die-cut sign on their railway cars or service vehicles in the era around 1930; 12" x 14", $300. *Courtesy of Bill and Belinda Fraser.*

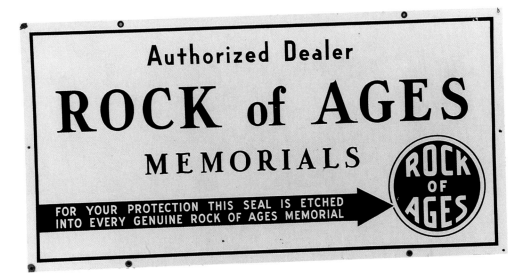

If size is your thing, you'll like this large Rock of Ages Memorials sign; c. 1950s, approximately 7" x 3.5", $800. *Courtesy of Crockett Blacklock.*

This oval Grapette Soda sign is a product of the 1950s era; 17" x 10", $225. *Courtesy of Michael Villamagna.*

Holligsworth's Candies are shown in plain script; c. 1940s, 36" x 12", $350. *Courtesy of Michael Villamagna.*

This small Dr. Pepper sign was possibly designated for use on a cooler; c. late 1950s, 13" x 5", $75. *Courtesy of Michael Villamagna.*

Veribrite Signs of Chicago, New York, and Dallas were the distributors for this REA Motor Transport sign; c. 1930s, 17" x 17", $350. *Courtesy of John Bobroff.*

A.J. Robinson and Son wanted you to know that their milk and cream came from "Tuberculin Tested Herds." This sign originated from Roslindale, Massachusetts; c. 1930s, 30", $600. *Courtesy of John Bobroff.*

This beautiful Purity Ice Cream stand-up sidewalk sign dates from the 1930s. Many of the signs pictured in this book were also designed to be used in similar type sidewalk stands; $950. *Author's Collection.*

Lorillard Company was the promoter of this "Between The Acts Cigars" sign; c. 1930s, 30" x 46", $1,000. *Courtesy of Michael Villamagna.*

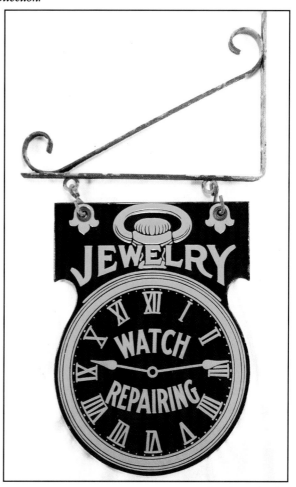

Here's another jewelry sign similar to the one found previously in this chapter. Complete with bracket, this generic sign could be used by most any business selling jewelry or repairing watches; c. 1930, approximately 14" x 26", $500. *Courtesy of Michael Villamagna.*

Sweet and Pure Flour is given center stage; c. 1930s, 28" x 9", $550. *Author's Collection.*

Commemorative signs were placed along the highways that were part of the original Santa Fe Trail to recognize its significance in the American highway system leading to the west; c. 1930s, $500. *Courtesy of Terry Stady.*

Although this sign appears to be a product of Scotland, it's actually quite American. Caledonian Insurance Company was originally founded in Scotland in 1805 and set up operations in America in the nineteenth century. The flowers at the bottom left are very unusual insomuch as they were hand-brushed onto the sign before it was fired. The small print at the bottom reads, "B.S. Company, 9th & Cherry Philadelphia and Harvey Ill;" 22" x 16", $500. *Author's Collection.*

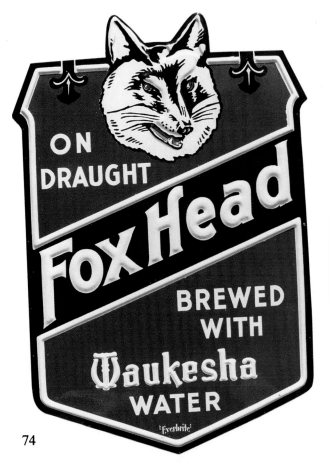

The sentiment this particular sign inspires makes it priceless. It was discovered in a final clean-out under my father's front porch in 1995, completely painted over. What a thrill it was to find such a legacy given to me by my father in such an unusual way; c. 1940, 16" x 9". Mine is priceless! Others, $250. *Author's Collection.*

Waukesha, Wisconsin, was the home of Fox Head Beer. This beautiful, die-cut sign was designed to be hung from a bracket; c. 1930s, approximately 26" x 38", $1,200. *Author's Collection.*

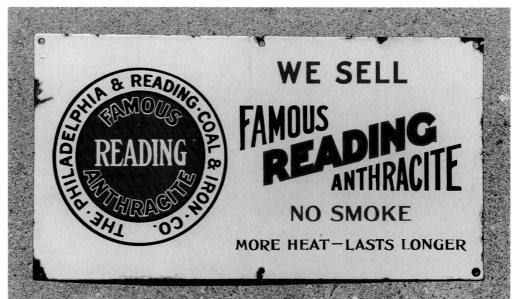

Thousands of American homes were heated by coal up until the 1960s. This famous Reading Anthracite sign was produced for attention in the home heating market; c. 1930s, 21" x 11", $250. *Courtesy of John Bobroff.*

Planters Fertilizer Phosphate was an animal byproduct This somewhat unusual example features a skeleton as its central logo. It was manufactured by Baltimore Enamel; c. 1940, $500. *Author's Collection.*

Here's another example of a sign targeted at the home heating market. Its outstanding graphics get the message across. It was manufactured by Veribrite Signs, Chicago; c. 1930, approximately 16" x 12", $700. *Author's Collection.*

Overall signs are popular among today's advertising collectors; c. 1930, 14" x 6", $675. *Author's Collection.*

Here's another variation on Castle Gate's theme, this particular one showing the sun coming up over the Wasatch Mountains of Utah; approximately 30" x 13", $600. *Author's Collection.*

Many American businesses were large enough to have their own emergency first aid department. This two-sided American Red Cross sign may have been placed in a large department store, a factory, or even a location such as a ski resort; c. 1940, 24" x 18", $175. *Courtesy of Shawn David.*

Art deco inspired the graphics of this Concordia Creamery sign; c. 1930s, approximately 48" x 12", $550. *Author's Collection.*

Boston Smoker Cigars are advertised on this strip sign; c. 1920s, $250. *Courtesy of Kim and Mary Kokles.*

Another variation on the cigar theme is R.G. Sullivan's 7-20-4 Cigar strip sign dating from the same era; approximately 22" x 3", $250. *Courtesy of Kim and Mary Kokles.*

Southern Belle brand wieners made a packaged die-cut image on this 1950s sign; approximately 24" x 24", $700. *Courtesy of Joe Pete Forcher.*

Southern Belle also produced this Hickory Smoked Ham die-cut sign in the 1950s; approximately 20" x 30", $700. *Courtesy of Joe Pete Forcher.*

Mayer Custom Made Shoes advertised on this sign dating from the 1920s; $350. *Courtesy of Darryl Tilden.*

Although it has little to say, the Cook's Paint picture is worth a thousand words; c. 1940s, 30", $400. *Courtesy of David Belcher.*

This small McCormick-Deering Farmall sign was no doubt used on an implement. Although its patent date of July 17, 1923, is displayed on the sign, the manufacturing process of the sign indicates a somewhat newer vintage, possibly as late as the 1940s; $350. *Courtesy of Larry Schrof.*

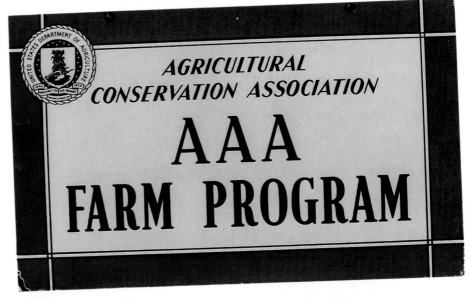

The Meadowlake Man is seen at his best on this sign. Notice that Meadowlake went to the trouble of making the tops of the bottles yellow, the only yellow on the entire sign; c. 1950, $450. *Courtesy of Harold and Donna Huddleston.*

The Agricultural Conservation Association used this AAA Farm Program sign in the 1930s. It is two-sided and designed to be hung from a bracket; $175. *Courtesy of Tom and Sherry Watt.*

Although this Mt. Hood Stages sign may have seen better days, phenomenal graphics warrant its inclusion here. It was designed to be hung from a bracket; c. 1930, 24" x 17", $1,000. *Courtesy of Tom Licouris.*

The City of Anchorage produced this small sign for placement on municipal trucks. Although it is dated on the obverse November 23, 1920, it was actually manufactured in the 1940s and '50s; 12", $150. *Courtesy of Rod Krupka.*

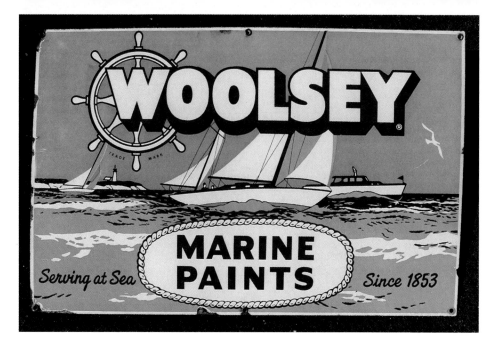

Beautiful graphics make this Woolsey Marine Paint sign first class; approximately 28" x 20", $675. *Private Collection.*

Ice cream signs are a popular subject matter and are actually a collectible in themselves; c. 1930s, $500. *Courtesy of Don Mangells.*

Here's another example from the long list of ice cream signs. This time from Hoffman's, which was a subsidiary of Sealtest; $500. *Courtesy of Don Mangells.*

79

American Indians have long been a popular collecting theme. Colorado Fence used an Indian chief in full head dress as the logo for their products; c. 1930s, approximately 20" x 17", $600. *Author's Collection.*

This interesting Experimental Radio Reporting Weather Station sign was no doubt located in a remote area. Leupold & Stevens were large manufacturers of many types of electronic instruments; c. 1940s, approximately 20" x 40", $450. *Author's Collection.*

Lehigh Valley was one of the United States' largest producers of residential coal; c. 1940s, approximately 14" x 11", $150. *Courtesy of Rod Krupka.*

The United States Forest Service used this small, die-cut shield sign in the 1930s. Its exact use is uncertain, but possibly it was found on Forest Service trucks; 4" x 5", $150. *Courtesy of Rod Krupka.*

This Alta Crest Farms sign dates to around 1930; approximately 24", $1,000. *Courtesy of Larry Schrof.*

Weiler Sterling Farms Company produced this beauty in the 1930s; approximately 24", $1,600. *Courtesy of Dale Brown.*

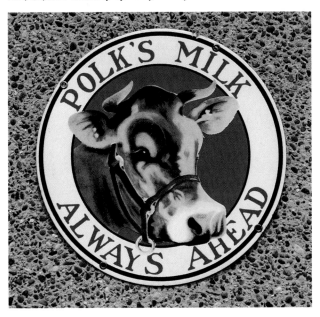

What a beauty this is! Polk's Milk would be hard pressed to find a more graphic way to catch the public eye than with this sign manufactured for use on the sides of trucks; c. 1930s, approximately 15", $2,000. *Courtesy of Larry Schrof.*

Madison, Wisconsin, is a logical place for this Universal Cleaners & Dryers sign; c. 1940, approximately 12" x 12", $300. *Courtesy of Larry Schrof.* Chapter 02/149

DeLaval was the largest manufacturer of cream separators in the world; c. 1930s, $700. *Courtesy of Larry Schrof.*

Ayrshire Cattle are the theme of this Alta Crest Farm sign; c. 1930s, $600. *Courtesy of Larry Schrof.*

Nevada Bell Telephone Company produced very few telephone signs through the years. This rare example dates to the early 1900s and is possibly one of a kind; $2,000. *Courtesy of Frank Feher.*

This Report Forest Fires Here sign dates from the 1920s; approximately 10" x 10", $250. *Author's Collection.*

Aboline, Texas, was the home of Banner Ice; c. 1940s, 24" x 14", $150. *Courtesy of John Bobroff.*

These two Lackawanna Anthracite signs are advertising coal to the public; c. 1935, 12", $250. *Courtesy of John Bobroff.*

The latter part of the nineteenth century saw this Hartford Fire Insurance Agency sign in service. It was manufactured by Imperial Enamel Company Limited, which was located in England, with an office in New York; 18" x 12", $400. *Courtesy of John Bobroff.*

There's nothing like the slogan found at the bottom of this Franklin Fire Insurance Company sign to put a little doubt in your mind; c. 1920s, 20" x 14", $400. *Courtesy of John Bobroff.*

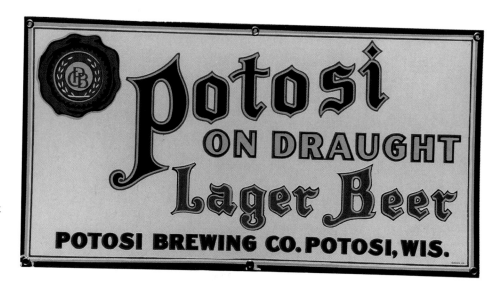

This large Morton Salt sign originated in Redding, California; c. 1930s, 48" x 18", $500. *Courtesy of John Bobroff.*

Potosi Lager Beer was one of the larger manufacturers of beer in Wisconsin in the 1930s. This sign was distributed by Burdick of Chicago; 21" x 11", $250. *Courtesy of John Bobroff.*

Earl Maddox, Jr. Ice Service used this for advertising; c. 1950s, 24", $400. *Courtesy of John Bobroff.*

The 1930s saw this Vulcanite Cement sign in service; 17" x 17", $150. *Courtesy of John Bobroff.*

This Pomona Bus Lines sign dates to around 1950; 27" x 15", $400. *Courtesy of John Bobroff.*

This Ridder Farms sign is a stand out. Some of the most beautiful graphics ever put into porcelain are found on dairy signs. Ridder Farms was located in Whitman, Massachusetts; c. 1930s, 24", $600. *Courtesy of John Bobroff.*

This Franklin Fire Insurance Company sign was used in the 1920s. The ink stamping at bottom right reads, "Brilliant Mfg. Co. PA;" 19" x 13", $400. *Courtesy of John Bobroff.*

The U.S. Forest Service sign shown here may have been used near a large tool box. These containers held such necessities for fire fighting as shovels and rakes. It was probably mounted on two wooden posts as evidenced by the grommet pattern; c. 1930s, 14" x 5", $150. *Courtesy of John Bobroff.*

This Garland Stoves and Ranges sign was designed to be hung from a bracket. The ink stamping at the bottom reads, "FMB Co. 52 State Street, Chicago, IL;" c. 1905, 24" x 24", $750. *Courtesy of John Bobroff.*

Ives Ice Cream is seen on this sidewalk stand; c. 1935, $800. *Courtesy of Country Charm Antiques.*

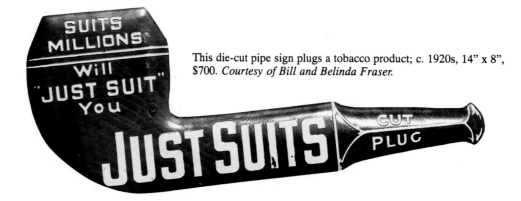

This die-cut pipe sign plugs a tobacco product; c. 1920s, 14" x 8", $700. *Courtesy of Bill and Belinda Fraser.*

This apartments sign has the capability of using interchangeable numbers as evidenced by the slots found on each side of the numbers. This would indicate how many rooms were available for rent; c. 1930, 16" x 18", $550. *Courtesy of Bill and Belinda Fraser.*

Burdan's Ice Cream was manufactured by Philadelphia Dairy Products Company. This two-sided sign was designed to be used in the usual sidewalk stand; c. 1940, $600. *Courtesy of Sam Ezell.*

It is interesting to note the similarities in some signs. Compare this Public Service No Smoking sign with the one found on page 32 of my first *Porcelain Enamel Advertising* book. No doubt the same manufacturer designed both; $850. *Courtesy of Bill and Belinda Fraser.*

Western Pacific's Feather River Route is advertised here; c. 1930, 24" x 22", $750. *Courtesy of Bill and Belinda Fraser.*

One of America's most familiar soft drinks is seen on this 7-Up sign; c. 1950s, approximately 24" x 10", $350. *Courtesy of Roger Blad.*

The image of Lawrence Barrett is found true to life on this cigar sign, produced by the lithographic process around the year 1915. The ink stamping at bottom reads, "BS Co. 166 North State Street, Chicago;" 41" x 18", $1,200. *Courtesy of Gene and Red Sonnen.*

The image of Reddy Kilowatt is the focus of this Central Illinois Public Service sign dating from the 1950s. This sign was photographed in service on a power company building located in Mt. Sterling, Illinois; $500. *Courtesy of Central Illinois Public Service Company.*

This is the kind of item that dreams are made of. Eveready would have to think hard to come up with a more eye-catching design than this; c. 1935, 18" x 34", $3,000. *Courtesy of Gene and Red Sonnen.*

Chapter Three

Flanged Two-Sided Signs

All signs in this chapter were designed with a built-in, side-mount flange. Normally this amounts to no more than a ninety-degree bend on one side of the sign. There are some other things that have shown up, though, such as the split-flange system used on some Western Union signs. Sometimes the only damage to the sign will be limited to the flange area. Unless it is severe, this should not count heavily in the grading or value of a sign. The face of the sign has the advertising, not the flange. Be careful to inspect flat, two-sided signs as they may prove to have been a flanged sign than had the flange carefully cut off. Normally, small chips will follow the edge that the saw blade went along and no porcelain will be evident along the edge as well.

Red Steer Brand fertilizers produced this beautiful die-cut sign in the 1930s; approximately 18" x 28", $800. *Courtesy of Larry Schrof.*

BPS produced this flanged sign around 1930. It is unusual insofar as each side has a different advertisement; approximately 15" x 22", $600. *Author's Collection.*

Michigan State Telephone Company was the predecessor to Michigan Bell and was in business until about 1923. This rare example dates from around 1905; 16" x 16", $900. *Courtesy of Mick Hoover.*

The familiar shape of a milk can comes to life on this die-cut Harding Cream Company sign; c. 1920s, approximately 16" x 24", $1,200. *Author's Collection.*

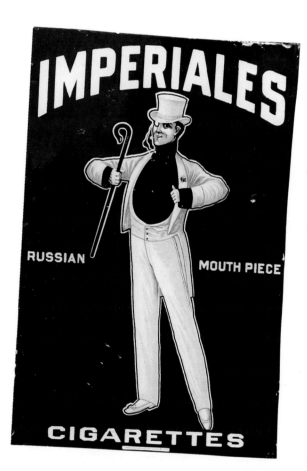

Imperiales Cigarettes' dapper man stands proud in an image created through the use of the lithographic process. It was manufactured by Balto Enamel; c. 1925, 16" x 23", $850. *Author's Collection.*

The image of the sun at the top right of this Sun Proof Paint sign was produced by using a fired-on decal. The rest of the sign was manufactured with a stencil; c. 1925, approximately 15" x 12", $600. *Author's Collection.*

Chase & Sanborn Coffee and Tea produced this Seal Brand sign in the 1920s; approximately 16" x 15", $250. *Courtesy of Harold and Donna Huddleston.*

This rare Tri-County Telephone Company sign dates to around 1925; 18" x 18", $1,000. *Private Collection.*

Interstate Utilities Company produced this Pay Station sign, distributed by Burdick of Chicago; c. 1930, 14" x 19", $1,200. *Courtesy of Denis and Jeanie Weber.*

Cream separators were big business on farms through the first half of this century. This large DeLaval Authorized Agency sign features their well-known separator; c. 1935, 21" x 32", $1,100. *Author's Collection.*

Stove and range signs have some of the most beautiful graphics found on any country store advertising. This Favorite Stoves and Ranges sign is no exception; c. 1915, approximately 20" x 29", $900. *Author's Collection.*

Keen Kutter was prominent in America's tool and cutlery business for years. Consequently it has become extremely desirable in the collectibles market. This die-cut, flanged sign features their logo; c. 1920, $1,300. *Courtesy of Kim and Mary Kokles.*

Cletrac was manufactured by the Cleveland Tractor Company, which produced this beautiful die-cut sign around 1935; approximately 28" x 22", $2,000. *Courtesy of Larry Schrof.*

This telephone sign has its origins in Canada. Notice the word "telephone" at top and "public" at bottom. This seemingly reversed sequence of words was used on many Canadian signs due to the necessity of French-English translation; c. 1940s, approximately 6" x 13", $250. *Courtesy of Mick Hoover.*

Had they stayed in business to the 1940s, the Southeastern Express corporate logo may have become somewhat unpopular; c. 1915, 12" x 10", $500. *Courtesy of Bill and Belinda Fraser.*

Although the condition is a little rough, the outstanding graphics on this H.W. Johns' Paint sign still warrants inclusion in this book. As you can see, the flange has been flattened and the sign was likely used to fill a hole in a wall somewhere. Unfortunately, it took the sign from a Grade 8 to a 5 in about 15 minutes. Even so, it still is a spectacular-looking piece; $200. *Courtesy of Fox & Hounds Antique Mall.*

Climax Plug did big business when this sign was manufactured around 1930; approximately 18" x 8", $275. *Courtesy of Bill and Belinda Fraser.*

Tremont Stoves and Ranges used this sign, manufactured by Ing-Rich of Beaver Falls, Pennsylvania; c. 1910, 13" x 13", $375. *Courtesy of Richard Merriman.*

These two Cash for Cream signs show you the similarities found
among many porcelain advertising signs. Both measure approximately 18" x 30" and were no doubt made by the same manufacturer; $300 each. *Courtesy of John Bobroff.*

Here's another example of a sign with different advertising on each
side. Sherwin-Williams must have figured that they would be
getting twice as much advertising in the same space; c. 1925,
approximately 24" x 18", $575. *Author's Collection.*

The American Agricultural Chemical
Company produced this sign around 1930;
approximately 22", $275. *Courtesy of
Princine Petinga.*

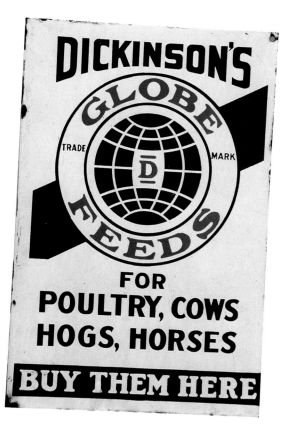

Farm signs are always popular advertising
items, like this Globe Feeds sign; c. 1930,
approximately 14" x 22", $450. *Author's
Collection.*

The list of beautifully manufactured
porcelain signs seems to go on and on. This
outstanding Helmar Turkish Cigarettes sign
features a die-cut, lithographed woman; c.
1920, approximately 16.5" x 23.5", $1,500.
Courtesy of John Romagnoli.

Star Tobacco. Plain and simple; c. 1910,
approximately 18" x 8", $300. *Courtesy of
Tom Licouris.*

Sherwin-Williams Paints' famous logo is found large on this "Cover The Earth" sign; c. 1940, 18" x 20", $750. *Courtesy of Tom Licouris.*

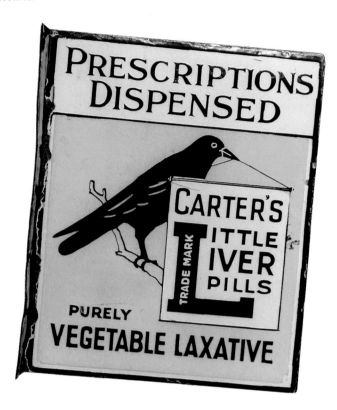

This Carter's Little Liver Pills sign was in service around 1915; 15" x 18", $400. *Courtesy of Pete Keim.*

Martin-Senour used this Paints & Varnishes Sold Here sign in the 1920s; approximately 22" x 16", $500. *Courtesy of Dick Marrah.*

Murad produced this Turkish Cigarette sign around 1920. What a work of art! The beautiful graphics found on the woman and cigarette package were created using the lithographic process; $1,700. *Courtesy of Lee and Bonnie Kollorz.*

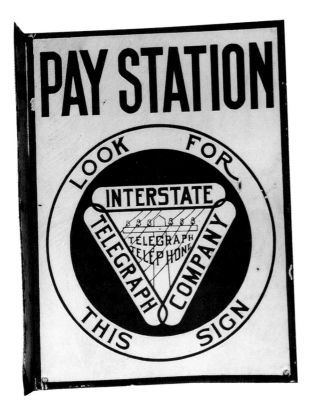

Many advertisers wanted their product to be a stand out on their signs. A case in point would be this beautiful Duke's Mixture sign; c 1925, 14.5" x 11", $650. *Courtesy of Pete Keim.*

Interstate Telegraph Company was an independent telephone utility. The Pay Station sign shown here incorporates their logo in its central image; c. 1920s, 12" x 16", $500. *Courtesy of Mick Hoover.*

Arden's Sunfreze Ice Cream is the theme of this sign; c. 1930, 18" x 22", $1,000. *Courtesy of Layne Christensen.*

This City Directory sign dates from the 1920s; 14" x 11", $400. *Courtesy of John Romagnoli.*

Any advertising from Wells Fargo & Company scores big with western collectors; c. 1895, approximately 28" x 14", $3,500. *Courtesy of Bill and Belinda Fraser.*

This Independent Telephone sign was used as a generic advertisement for many small telephone operations throughout the country; c. 1930s, approximately 17" x 18", $600. *Courtesy of Mick Hoover.*

Although this Red Dry Seal Battery sign was produced in quantity, few remain in the condition seen here. The battery terminal at the top left is normally either missing or severely damaged with the balance of the sign getting pelted by those making sure their aim is still good; c. 1930, 13" x 24.5", $450. *Courtesy of John Romagnoli.*

Here's one more example of an advertising sign doing double time. The International Clothes sign on the left is on the opposite side of the International Tailoring advertisement at the right; c. 1920s, approximately 22" x 17", $650. *Courtesy of Bill and Belinda Fraser.*

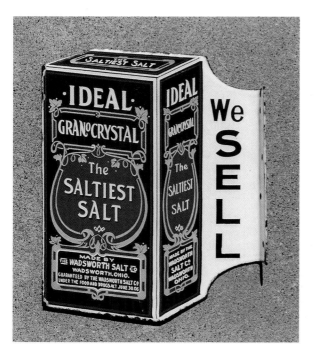

Ingram-Richardson manufactured this small Ideal Salt sign, ink stamped "Ingram-Richardson, Beaver Falls, PA" on the flange; c. 1910, 10" x 12", $1,500. *Courtesy of Pete Keim.*

The beautiful graphics created on this Dutch Boy Brand White Lead sign were created by using the lithographic process. As evidenced by the ink stamp at bottom left, it may have been manufactured in 1916; approximately 16" x 24", $800. *Courtesy of Dave and Kathy Lane.*

Singer Sewing Machines used this logo for years and years. There are small differences, though, in the appearance of the woman. These can be mostly noted by the appearance of her face. A quantity of these signs were discovered recently and have all been absorbed into the collectors' market. The sign shown here measures approximately 15" x 24"; $1,100. *Courtesy of Tom and Susan Dahl.*

The State of Arkansas is silhouetted on this Public Telephone sign dating from the 1950s. It is unusual with its green color scheme; approximately 12" x 14", $600. *Courtesy of Denis and Jeanie Weber.*

Although this Alta Crest Farms sign appears normal at first glance, the accompanying photograph of its reverse side reveals a most unusual piece. The normal process for one-sided signs would not include a flange. However, because of the particular mounting situation required by Alta Crest Farms, a flange was necessary but advertising on the reverse was not. Close examination of the cow's expression seems to indicate it was posing for the artist; $650. *Courtesy of Tim and Leevona Blair.*

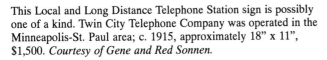

This Local and Long Distance Telephone Station sign is possibly one of a kind. Twin City Telephone Company was operated in the Minneapolis-St. Paul area; c. 1915, approximately 18" x 11", $1,500. *Courtesy of Gene and Red Sonnen.*

Cook's Paint & Varnishes advertised themselves "Best for Wear and Weather;" c. 1940, 18", $200. *Courtesy of Tim and Leevona Blair.*

SWEET-ORR TROUSERS THE BEST

Sweet-Orr produced this two-color sign
around 1930; 18" x 10", $400. *Courtesy of
Bill and Belinda Fraser.*

NOONAN'S HAIR PETROLE FOR FALLING HAIR

This unusual Noonan's Hair Petrole sign
dates from the 1940s; 16" x 14", $350.
Courtesy of Bill and Belinda Fraser.

AGENCY FOR IHC LINE — TRADE MARK

The IHC Line Agency had this sign in
service in the 1930s; 14" x 20", $300.
Courtesy of Bill and Belinda Fraser.

NORTHWESTERN TELEPHONE EXCHANGE CO. PAY STATION — LOCAL AND LONG DISTANCE TELEPHONE

Northwestern Telephone Exchange Company used this Pay Station
sign around 1915; 23" x 8.5", $750. *Courtesy of Gene and Red
Sonnen.*

Chapter Four

Curved Signs

This chapter contains signs that were designed to go around something. Normally, this would be the corner of a building. This was quite common during the early part of this century. A special mounting bracket was employed to the corner of the building and the sign fastened to the bracket. Curved signs had other uses as well, such as being found on telephone poles or streetlight posts. Some companies had their curved signs tailor-fit to go right on the product being advertised. As an example, a root beer sign would be fastened to a dispenser. We will also find some signs which are circular, not perfectly flat. These are nicknamed hubcaps by collectors.

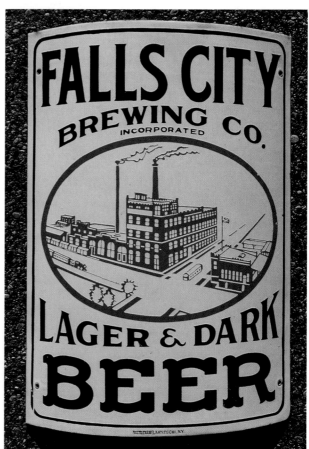

Baltimore Enamel & Novelty Company manufactured this outstanding Falls City Brewing Company sign. Its central image incorporates graphics depicting their operations which include a streetcar and train of that era; c. 1910, approximately 16" x 25", $1,300. *Author's Collection.*

Burdick Enamel Sign Company of Chicago and Baltimore distributed this beautiful Oshkosh Beer sign. Chief Oshkosh proudly stands as the center image; c. 1920s, 18", $750. *Courtesy of Gene and Red Sonnen.*

This hubcap from Arkansas Western Gas Company was manufactured in the 1950s; 6", $200. *Courtesy of Denis and Jeanie Weber.*

Admiration Coffee used this small curved sign some time in the 1920s; approximately 4" x 5", $275. *Courtesy of Harold and Donna Huddleston.*

This Kernan Stove Furnaces & Ranges curved sign was in use around 1905; approximately 16" x 28", $750. *Courtesy of W.K. Richards.*

Golden State Beer advertised its Milwaukee Brewery in San Francisco on this curved corner sign. The central image of this beauty was done with a lithographic process and features some of the basic ingredients found in their product; c. 1905, $1,200. *Courtesy of Kim and Mary Kokles.*

Piedmont Cigarettes were an eastern seaboard favorite for years; c. 1930, 14" x 17", $800. *Author's Collection.*

Brilliant Manufacturing Company produced this Crown Furnaces and Ranges sign. Its beautiful lettering combined with the photograph on porcelain of their stove make this sign a standout; c. 1915, $650. *Author's Collection.*

Fancy color schemes aren't necessary to get the message across as demonstrated by this Columbia Bicycles Agency sign; c. 1920, approximately 13" x 20", $700. *Courtesy of Dave and Kathy Lane.*

Wichita's Best Flour is shown big on this sign distributed by Burdick of Chicago; c. 1920s, 16" x 25", $800. *Courtesy of Dave and Kathy Lane.*

Here's one of the finest porcelain advertising pieces ever produced. Its country store charm sets the example in porcelain enamel advertising; c. 1920s, approximately 18" x 26", Rare. *Courtesy of Gary Metz.*

Sun-Proof Paints produced the unusual graphics seen on this sign; c. 1920, 20" x 22", $475. *Courtesy of Vic and Sara Raupe.*

This Campbell's Soup sign is an outstanding example of country store advertising. An identical sign was also manufactured with the word "tomato" replacing the word "vegetable;" c. 1920s, approximately 13" x 22.5", $2,000. *Courtesy of Pete Keim.*

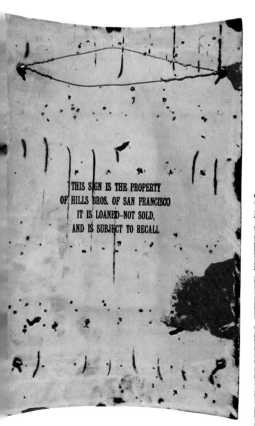

THIS SIGN IS THE PROPERTY OF HILLS BROS. OF SAN FRANCISCO IT IS LOANED–NOT SOLD, AND IS SUBJECT TO RECALL

Here's a shot of the back side of one of the Hills Brothers signs. Occasionally porcelain signs would be stamped with a similar marking asking for the return of the sign when not in use. This was the exception, not the rule, as most companies figured their advertising signs were going on a one-way trip. *Courtesy of Pete Keim.*

This gorgeous trio of Hills Brothers signs represents all of the known curved signs manufactured for Hills Brothers; c. 1910, 11" x 18", $1,500 each. *Courtesy of Pete Keim.*

It is difficult to imagine how Brattleboro Overall Company of Keene, New Hampshire, could have made this sign more appealing. The running brakeman combined with the locomotive in motion brings the sign to life. For overall graphic eye appeal, this is as good as it gets; c. 1915, approximately 15" x 22", Rare. *Courtesy of Robert Newman.*

How do you top this? Red-Top Flour was manufactured in St. Joseph, Missouri, in the early part of the twentieth century. This beautiful, curved example has their logo done by the lithograph process; approximately 16" x 22", $5,500. *Courtesy of Pete Keim.*

This curved Ranier Beer sign is one of a long list of identically shaped beer signs dating from the era between 1900 and 1925; 20" x 15", $500. *Courtesy of Pete Keim.*

Here's a close-up shot of the fired-on dating on the reverse side of the Ranier Beer sign. Unfortunately, this practice was somewhat uncommon because it was time consuming. However, we're fortunate that the company that manufactured this sign went to the trouble as now we can date the Ranier sign to the year 1908. *Courtesy of Pete Keim.*

This convex sign is typical of the outstanding graphics many signs used around 1905. Old Joe's Steam Beer was brewed in San Jose, California; 18", $1,200. *Courtesy of Pete Keim.*

Swift's Pride Soap went to the trouble of making the central image of this curved sign in black; $500. *Courtesy of Pete Keim.*

The lithographed bottle gives this sign added appeal. Fredericksburg Lager was brewed in San Francisco; c. 1900, approximately 13" x 20", $750. *Courtesy of Pete Keim.*

I couldn't resist showing you a close-up of the intricate work on the Fredericksburg Lager Beer sign. Sometimes I wonder if the artists hired at porcelain enamel manufacturers worked at the Bureau of Engraving and Printing first as demonstrated by the wonderful details seen here. *Courtesy of Pete Keim.*

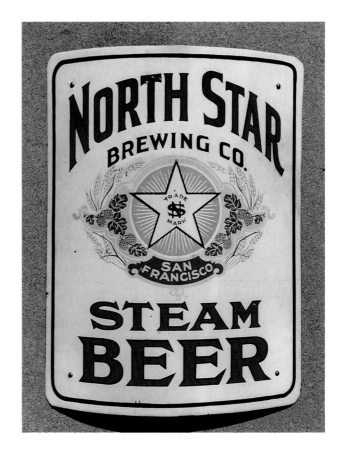

This convex Miller Milwaukee Beer sign was distributed by Burdick of Chicago sometime around 1910; 18", $400. *Courtesy of Pete Keim.*

North Star Steam Beer used fine graphics in its central image on this curved sign; c. 1905, 15" x 21", $700. *Courtesy of Pete Keim.*

Sweet, Orr & Company was one of the most prolific users of porcelain enamel advertising in this century; c. 1910, 18" x 14", $1,500. *Courtesy of Pete Keim.*

Here's a close-up of the central image on the Sweet Orr sign. The beautiful, color graphics were done with the lithographic process. *Courtesy of Pete Keim.*

Yosemite Lager produced this die-cut curved sign around 1905; 16" x 21", $1,500. *Courtesy of Pete Keim.*

Brassy & Company Kentucky Whiskeys were actually manufactured in San Jose, California. This example was distributed by Burdick of Chicago and B.E. & N. Company, 212 Sansome Street, San Francisco, sometime just after the turn of the century; 15" x 18", $500. *Courtesy of Pete Keim.*

Buffalo Brewing Company Lager was manufactured in Sacramento, California. Unfortunately the manufacturer of this beautiful sign is unknown; c. 1905, 13" x 20", $1,500. *Courtesy of Pete Keim.*

Burdick Sign Company of Chicago distributed this Ranier Beer sign around 1910; 16" x 23", $750. *Courtesy of Pete Keim.*

Pacific Club's Special Brew is advertised on this unusual oval curved sign manufactured by Ing-Rich of Beaver Falls, Pennsylvania; c. 1905. 15" x 20", $1,000. *Courtesy of Pete Keim.*

Western Union produced this convex Telephone-Telegrams sign in the 1920s; 8", $350. *Courtesy of Bill and Belinda Fraser.*

Sacramento, California, was the home of Ruhstaller Gilt Edge Beer. Baltimore Enamel and Novelty Company manufactured this sign sometime around 1910; 16" x 23", $1,000. *Courtesy of Pete Keim.*

Economy and quality are all that counts on this Schilling's Best sign; c. 1915, 9.5" x 14", $400. *Courtesy of Pete Keim.*

Chapter Five

Thermometers, Door Pushes, Trays, & Smalls

Many detective agencies were primarily in the business of commercial security. Small Jennings signs were no doubt placed near entrances on commercial buildings; c. 1920s, 4" x 4.5", $100. *Courtesy of Pete Keim.*

This Beech-Nut Tobacco sign was used as a door push; c. 1920s, 9" x 13", $500. *Courtesy of Tom Licouris.*

This Ingersoll Watch door push dates to around 1930; 3" x 6.5", $500. *Courtesy of Tom Licouris.*

Cubo Cigar produced this beautiful, slightly convex, die-cut door push in the 1920s; 8" x 2.5", $400. *Courtesy of Pete Keim.*

Star Naptha Washing Powder is featured on this door push dating from around 1915; 3.5" x 6.5", $200. *Courtesy of Pete Keim.*

This Orange Crush door push dates to around 1935; 3.5" x 9.5", $350. *Courtesy of John Romagnoli.*

This Naptholeine strip sign dates from around 1905; 13.5" x 3", $250. *Courtesy of Pete Keim.*

The Denver and Ephrata Telephone Company sign pictured here may have been used on the sides of company trucks. The Denver and Ephrata Telephone Company was located in Pennsylvania; c. 1910, 5", $1,000. *Courtesy of Gene and Red Sonnen.*

Red Hat Motor Oil makes the grade on this outstanding thermometer dating from the 1920s; 20", $3,000. *Courtesy of Dave and Kathy Lane.*

This Local and Long Distance Telephone die-cut sign was undoubtedly used on a telephone booth; c. 1910, approximately 8" x 9", $650. *Courtesy of Denis and Jeanie Weber.*

This small Accident Tickets sign dates from around 1925; 7" x 3.5", $450. *Courtesy of Bill and Belinda Fraser.*

Syracuse, New York, was the home of Thomas Ryan's Ales & Lager. Their Indian chief logo makes a graphic impression on this beer tray dating from the 1920s; $450. *Author's Collection.*

One of America's most famous logos is seen on this door push from the 1930s. As you can see, not all door pushes will say "push;" $450. *Courtesy of Tom and Susan Dahl.*

Beautiful graphics make this Recruit Little Cigars door push a stand out. The H. Ellison Company of Baltimore, Maryland, produced this sign around 1915; 4" x 8.5", $600. *Courtesy of Pete Keim.*

This small Mayer Shoes door push dates from around the turn of the century; 3.5" x 5", $350. *Courtesy of Tom and Susan Dahl.*

Hubert Fischer Brewery had this beer tray manufactured sometime around 1915; $500. *Courtesy of Dick and Kathy Purvis.*

Due to health concerns, this small Spitting On The Floor sign was made for those needing a reminder; c. 1925, 8" x 4", $250. *Courtesy of Bill and Belinda Fraser.*

Duke's Mixture used this door push around 1915; 5.5" x 8", $450. *Courtesy of Pete Keim.*

The word "cures" on this Vapo-Cresolene sign would have been banned by the Pure Foods & Drugs Act of Congress in 1906. We'll date this sign, then, to the years just preceding the 1906 law; 12" x 5", $400. *Courtesy of Pete Keim.*

Jap Rose Soap is featured on this strip sign; c. 1920, 15" x 3", $300. *Courtesy of Pete Keim.*

This beautiful Polar Bear Tobacco door push dates from around 1910; 3.5" x 7.5", $600. *Courtesy of Pete Keim.*

Napa Soda Lemonade is seen on this sign dating from around 1910; 7" x 5", $500. *Courtesy of Pete Keim.*

The central image on this New England Brewing Company Ales & Lager beer tray was done in black and white lithography; c. 1910, $600. *Courtesy of Dick and Kathy Purvis.*

"For The Wise One" is the slogan for this B-L Cut Plug door push; c. 1910, 8" x 12", $500. *Courtesy of Pete Keim.*

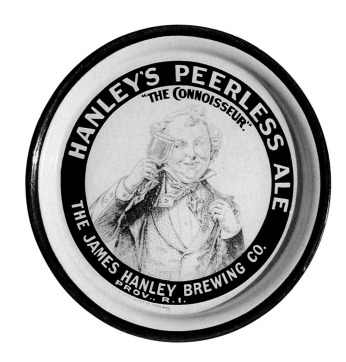

This die-cut door push advertising Majors Cement dates to around 1915; 3" x 7.5", $125. *Courtesy of Pete Keim.*

The James Hanley Brewing Company of Providence, Rhode Island, used this lithographed Hanley's Peerless Ale beer tray around 1905. The beautiful graphics were done in lithograph and feature "The Connoisseur". It was manufactured in England by an unknown company; $800. *Courtesy of Dick and Kathy Purvis.*

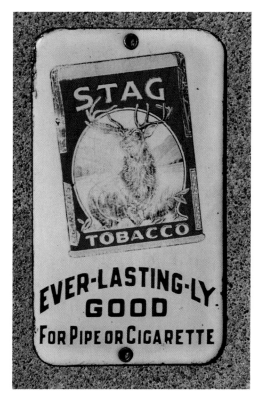

Chesterfield Cigarettes used this door push in the era around 1930; 4" x 9", $350. *Courtesy of Pete Keim.*

Stag Tobacco used this beautiful, door push with a 100 percent lithographed package; c. 1910; 4" x 6.5", $300. *Courtesy of Pete Keim.*

This small Mail Pouch Tobacco sign dates from around 1920; $150. *Courtesy of Michael Villamagna.*

Red Man Tobacco is seen on this door push dating from around 1915; 3" x 6", $150. *Courtesy of Pete Keim.*

This beautiful Aetna Brewing Company beer tray dates to around 1915; $600. *Courtesy of Dick and Kathy Purvis.*

Polar Ware pushed up sales with this ashtray manufactured sometime around 1930; 5", $60. *Author's Collection.*

This small Home Comfort Ranges & Furnaces advertisement is big on graphics. The detail work, if studied carefully, reveals a true work of art; c. late 1800s, approximately 6" x 4", $250. *Courtesy of Pete Keim.*

Along with the three curved signs found previously in this book, Hills Brothers Tea & Coffee also produced this small door push around 1915; 4" x 6.5", $500. *Courtesy of Pete Keim.*

Here's a real museum piece. The lithographed image of a messenger on the American District Telegraph door push is a stand out in anyone's book; c. 1900; 5.5" x 8.5", $1,900. *Courtesy of Pete Keim.*

This close-up shot of the American District Telegraph messenger reveals the fine artwork involved in the lithographic process. Notice that such details as the individual strands of hair on the boy and the shadows throughout his uniform give a natural appearance. This kind of workmanship is truly unsurpassed. *Courtesy of Pete Keim.*

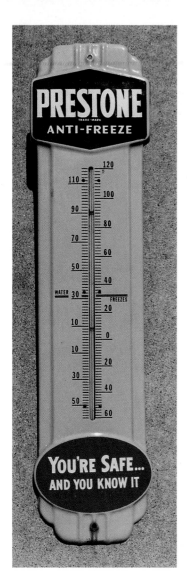

It must have been a time-consuming job to produce all the colors required for this Canadian Luxor Paint thermometer; c. 1940, $800. *Courtesy of Dick and Kathy Purvis.*

This Prestone Anti-Freeze thermometer is of 1940s vintage. It was manufactured in the thousands, but a fair number that remain are considerably damaged. This example is definitely the exception; $200. *Author's Collection.*

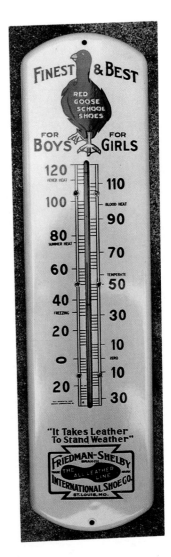

Hubert Fischer Brewery had this Lager Beer tray produced for them sometime around 1915; $700. *Courtesy of Dick and Kathy Purvis.*

Red Goose Shoes is a favorite name among country store advertising collectors; c. 1930, $475. *Author's Collection.*

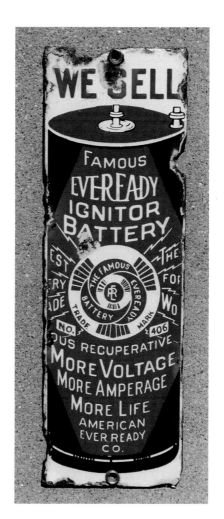

Although the *Porcelain Enamel Encyclopedia* limits its items to those produced for North American Advertising, this European Singer Sewing Machines thermometer was included because of its fine use of graphics and color, typical of many signs produced overseas; c. 1935, approximately 7" x 40", $1,700. *Courtesy of W.K. Richards.*

Although this Eveready Ignitor Battery door push is a little bit rough around the edges, its beautiful graphics warrant inclusion here; c. 1925, 3.5" x 10.5", $250. *Courtesy of John Romagnoli.*

Door pushes were still big business even in the 1940s, when this Vicks Vat-Tro-Nol push was manufactured; 3.5" x 6.5", $200. *Courtesy of Michael Villamagna.*

Here's another door push on the Duke's Mixture theme; c. 1915, 5.5" x 8", $450. *Courtesy of Pete Keim.* $450

121

Beach of Coshocton, Ohio, was one of the largest advertising thermometer manufacturers in the world. This Hills Brothers Tea & Coffee thermometer was patented March 16, 1915; 9" x 21", $700. *Courtesy of Pete Keim.*

American Family Soap is seen on this door push; c. 1930, 4" x 8.5", $250. *Courtesy of Michael Villamagna.*

Nature's Remedy was big on thermometer advertising. This unusual 7" x 27" example dates from around 1930; $350. *Courtesy of John Romagnoli.*

These cute Tudor Tea signs measure a scant 4" x 3" each; c. 1910, $150. *Courtesy of Pete Keim.*

The beautiful graphics found on this Karo Household Syrup door push are a country store collector's delight; c. 1915, 4" x 6.5", $900. *Courtesy of Pete Keim.*

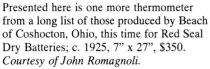

Presented here is one more thermometer from a long list of those produced by Beach of Coshocton, Ohio, this time for Red Seal Dry Batteries; c. 1925, 7" x 27", $350. *Courtesy of John Romagnoli.*

Coca-Cola produced hundreds of porcelain advertising pieces through the years; c. 1940s, 3.5" x 14", $375. *Courtesy of Michael Villamagna.*

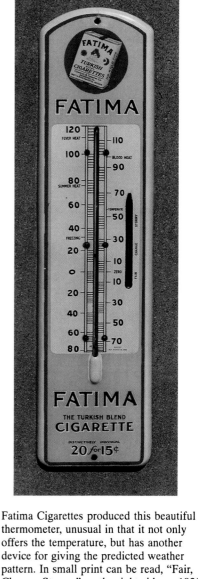

Fatima Cigarettes produced this beautiful thermometer, unusual in that it not only offers the temperature, but has another device for giving the predicted weather pattern. In small print can be read, "Fair, Change, Stormy" on the right side; c. 1920, 7" x 27", $650. *Courtesy of John Romagnoli.*

Here's one more on the Magic Yeast theme; c. 1915, 2" x 7", $75. *Courtesy of Pete Keim.*

Outstanding graphics are found on this Magic Yeast door push; c. 1915, 3" x 6", $300. *Courtesy of Pete Keim.*

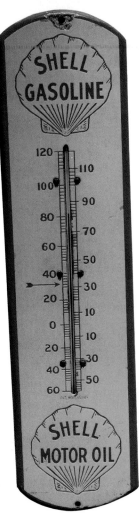

The advertising claims on this Coles Peruvian Bark and Wild Cherry Bitters sign might give one the idea that it could cure almost anything. Many products made such claims until 1906 when the Pure Food and Drug Act intervened; c. 1900, 16" x 6", $400. *Courtesy of Pete Keim.*

Beach of Coshocton, Ohio, manufactured this Shell Gas thermometer; c. 1925, 7" x 27", $2,000. *Courtesy of Tom Licouris.*

This Chew Smoke Mail Pouch strip sign was used in the 1920s; 18" x 3.5", $225. *Courtesy of Michael Villamagna.*

This beautiful Smith Brothers Ale beer tray seems to purport medicinal value; c. 1915, $850. *Courtesy of Dick and Kathy Purvis.*

Waterman & Leavitt produced this convenient match striker. They were distributors for Baltimore Enamel and Novelty Company in Boston. It has a granulated surface on the area at the bottom to ignite a match; c. 1915, 3" x 6", $400. *Courtesy of Pete Keim.*

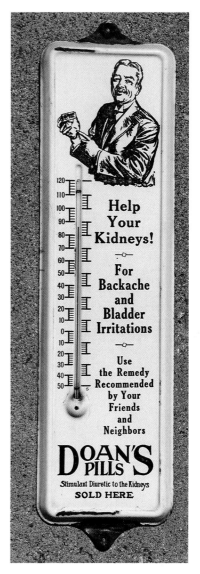

A large bottle of Stafford's Commercial Ink gives the necessary visual impact on this thermometer; c. 1925, 7" x 27", $500. *Courtesy of Pete Keim.*

This unusual Barber Shop sign contains a small thermometer. Despite the fact that it was manufactured in the 1920s, it's still going strong; $650. *Courtesy of Ernie Vigil.*

Here's an old product that works like new today—Doan's Pills' two-color thermometer; c. 1915, 6.5" x 24", $300. *Courtesy of John Bobroff.*

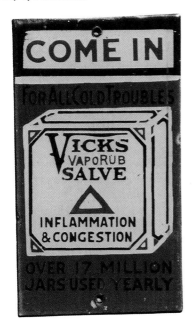

This unusual Vicks VapoRub Salve door push dates to around 1930; 4" x 6.5", $275. *Courtesy of John Romagnoli.*

This washroom sign dates from around 1930; 9" x 6", $300. *Courtesy of Pete Keim.*

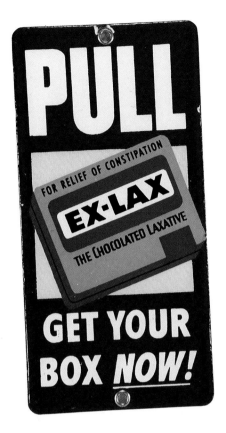

This Ex-Lax door push invokes a sense of urgency; c. 1940, 4" x 10", $175. *Courtesy of Michael Villamagna.*

This unusual oval 7-Up thermometer dates from the 1940s; 6" x 15", $125. *Courtesy of Michael Villamagna.*

Murphy Miles Fuel Oils used this thermometer in the 1930s; 3" x 12", $175. *Courtesy of Michael Villamagna.*

This Have a Coca-Cola door push is of Canadian origin; c. 1950s; 3.5" x 6.5", $325. *Courtesy of Michael Villamagna.*

OVB Hardware, Cutlery, Tools, and Paints is seen on this 3" x 8" door push; c. 1905, $125. *Courtesy of Pete Keim.*

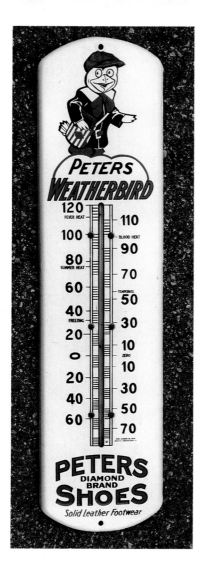

This Juicy Orange door push dates from the 1940s , 3.5" x 8", $175. *Courtesy of Michael Villamagna.*

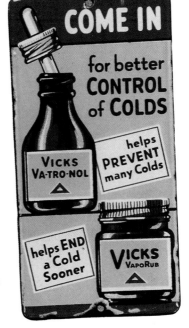

This great looking thermometer advertising Peters Weatherbird Shoes was manufactured by Beach of Coshocton, Ohio, around 1930; 8" x 27", $350. *Courtesy of Gene and Red Sonnen.*

Pollack Wheeling Stogies used this thermometer sometime around 1935; 8" x 35", $200. *Courtesy of Michael Villamagna.*

Vicks Control of Colds door push was in service around 1930; 4" x 8", $275. *Courtesy of John Romagnoli.*

The full-width Royal Crown Cola door push presented here was manufactured in the 1950s; 35" x 4", $200. *Courtesy of Michael Villamagna.*

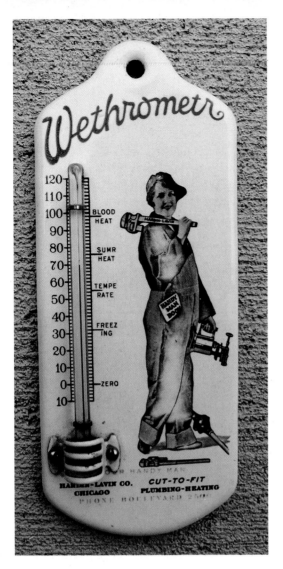

Hartmann Brewing Company produced this Lager, Ales & Porter beer tray around 1920; $450. *Courtesy of Dick and Kathy Purvis.*

Cut-to-Fit Plumbing and Heating is advertised on this lithographed thermometer; c. 1920, $550. *Courtesy of Tom and Susan Dahl.*

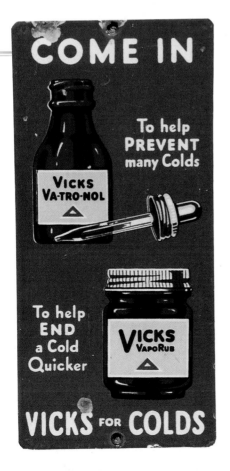

Here's one more in a long list of Vicks door pushes, this time with a red background; c. 1930, approximately 4" x 10", $175. *Courtesy of Lee and Bonnie Kollorz.*

Martin-Senour is one of the world's best-known paints. This may be due in part to the prolific amount of advertising in porcelain produced for them through the years. This two-color thermometer dates from around 1930; $250. *Courtesy of Dave and Kathy Lane.*

Chapter Six

A Porcelain Potpourri

Porcelain enamel advertising has come to mean more than just signs. The list of items produced over the years could fill a book in itself. Gum machines, pop dispensers, thermometers, ashtrays, and a lot more were all produced with the common factor of having a porcelain message. This chapter also contains signs still in service on buildings.

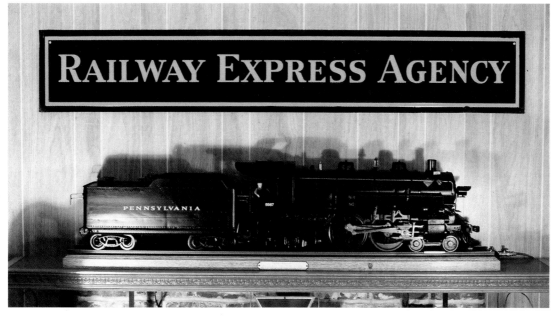

These two beauties are made for each other! The engine is hand built and one of a kind. However, the Railway Express Agency sign was made in fairly plentiful quantities. It dates to the 1920s and could be found at many local railway stations across America; approximately 10" x 5', $600. *Courtesy of Lee and Bonnie Kollorz.*

You never know what you'll find driving down back roads. Much to the author's surprise, this barrage of porcelain was plastered on these two buildings in Belle Plaine, Iowa. There are more than 100 signs on these buildings, most of which are in surprisingly good condition. Don't get any ideas, as just out of the photograph there are six pit bulls running loose in the yard.

Ford Motor Company produced this "Tractor" sign in the era before their logo became New Holland. It dates from the 1930s and is located here on a small shop in Maquoketa, Iowa.

This Nourse Motor Oils Lubester dates to around 1925. Its beautiful graphics were re-created by artist David Lane; $3,000. *Courtesy of Dave and Kathy Lane.*

Radio Service was big business until the 1960s. This Barnes Radio Service sign and its matching Car Radio Service sign above the garage door are tributes to the 1940s era when these were installed. They both still give faithful service in Reno, Nevada.

This small 3" x 5" call box was designed to be flush mounted on a wall. It is a combination call box insofar as Western Union and American District Telegraph had a cooperation contract for use of the same lines; $350. *Courtesy of Denis and Jeanie Weber.*

This huge Henneberg Furniture Company sign comes complete with a service ladder mounted right to the framework. It's located in Parkersburg, West Virginia.

Sometimes it's hard to imagine that signs like the one pictured here are still standing. This beautiful Poll Parott Brand Shoe sign is on a second story in downtown Springfield, Illinois. There is an identical sign just around the corner and, yes, the store still sells shoes.

This die-cut Emergency Road Service Station sign is in the original position where it was mounted more than forty years ago. It is located on a garage in Gardnerville, Nevada.

This I.F.C.A. Church sign was probably installed around 1940. It still stands in Fenton, Michigan.

131

Blumenthal's store is still doing big business in Greensboro, North Carolina. There are no fewer than eight porcelain signs on the building front, not including the gigantic multi-part sign over the entire store which measures at least 50 feet in length.

Daniel Boone Village in Hillsboro, North Carolina, is an antique mall that knows how to catch the public's attention. *Courtesy of Sam Ezell.*

This Prairie Trails Motel sign has a beautiful Conestoga wagon affixed to the top. The entire sign is done in neon which unfortunately has not been working for years. It is located near San Jose, Illinois.

Here's a front and reverse shot of the same root beer barrel dispenser. It is unusual insofar as there are not one, but two, porcelain signs mounted on it. In addition to this, neither one of the companies or products advertised on the signs seemed to be related, other than the fact that they are both root beer. Very different! $1,200. *Courtesy of Debbie Jackson.*

O.B. McClintock of Minneapolis, Minnesota, was one of the largest bank alarm manufacturers in the 1920s and '30s. This porcelain sign was designed to be placed conspicuously for obvious reasons. It is still giving service in Columbus, Wisconsin.

Early call boxes often had wood backboards. This American District Telegraph Messengers call box dates from the late 1800s. $600. *Courtesy of Denis and Jeanie Weber.*

These three small badges were used by employees for identification purposes. They are all porcelain on metal, manufactured with a technique called cloisonne. Thousands of badges and miscellaneous small items were manufactured through the years using this process because of its long-lasting properties. American Express Co. badge, $400; *courtesy of Bill and Belinda Fraser.* Postal Telegraph badge, $125; *courtesy of Denis and Jeanie Weber.* Tri-State Telephone shield, $300; *courtesy of Denis and Jeanie Weber.*

The 1930s was the era when this mortar and pestle was manufactured; 12" wide x 23" tall, $800. *Courtesy of Ernie Vigil.*

Carnation Malted Milk is found on this rare container dating from the 1920s; approximately 12" high including lid, $550. *Courtesy of Don Mangells.*

Thompson's Malted Milk was dispensed from this rare container sometime in the 1920s. Its pristine condition makes for plenty of collector appeal; $800. *Courtesy of Tom and Susan Dahl.*

Standard Oil Company of Indiana produced many of these lubesters in the era around 1920. This beautifully restored model would be a welcome addition to any petro collection; $1,000. *Courtesy of Dave and Kathy Lane.*

You could not even sit down without porcelain advertising being present. This Kabo Corsets seat dates from around 1910; $400. *Author's Collection.*

Chiclets used this slick looking Dentyne Gum machine in the 1930s. It was manufactured by Mills Automatic Merchandising Corporation of New York; 8" square x 32" high, $600. *Courtesy of Michael Villamagna.*

This Cattlemen's Association of Oklahoma sign is slowly being eaten by the tree that is supporting it. It was found as such on a dirt road in eastern Oklahoma.

There were dozens of lollipop type scales manufactured in the early part of this century. The beautiful example presented here was manufactured by Auto Scales Corporation of New York. It comes complete with porcelain marquee, and here sits high overlooking a valley in the home of Layne Christensen; c. 1910, $2,000. *Courtesy of Layne Christensen.*

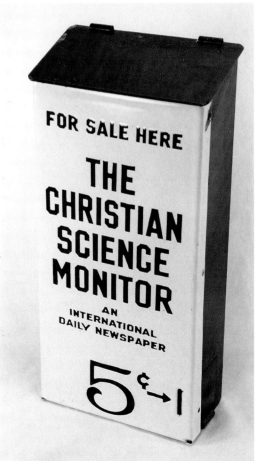

This Christian Science Monitor newspaper box was operated by inserting a coin at the bottom right. This released the latch on the door at the top and made the box's contents self-serve; 6.5" x 13", $225. *Courtesy of Michael Villamagna.*

Although not evident in the photograph, the Pangburn's Pure Food Ice Cream sign presented here is actually a corner sign, or rather, two identical signs angled 90 degrees from each other; c. 1920, 6" x 36", $2,000. *Courtesy of Layne Christensen.*

136

This large Packard sign still stands in Grass Valley, California, though its original neon tubing has long since disappeared.

Here's a Christmas decorating idea sure to please petro collectors. The garland-engulfed visible pump at left complements the beautiful six foot Iso-Vis thermometer at right. Both are to be enjoyed in this photograph taken in downtown Van Buren, Arkansas. *Courtesy of Randy Reith.*

Although partially stripped of its neon tubing, this Sam's Auto Parts sign is still giving faithful service in Hazel Park, Michigan.

A drive through the Adirondacks uncovered this handsome roadside pair. The fuel pump at left is complemented by the porcelain Socony Motor Oil Crank Case Service sign. *Courtesy of DeZalia and Sons Garage.*

Although this large Coca-Cola sign is a little rough around the edges, its rarity warrants inclusion here. It was designed to be used with neon as evidenced by the holes placed strategically throughout the sign; 10' x 4', $600. *Courtesy of School Time Antiques.*

These two neon Buick signs are still giving service at a dealership located in Mifflinburg, Pennsylvania; c. 1930s.

Neon lighting is still a functioning part of this Eagles Hall sign dating from the 1930s. It was captured here in action in Reynoldsville, Pennsylvania.

This Deep-Rock Gasoline and Motor Oils sign is the only reminder of a once-thriving service station in northeastern Wisconsin. Such reminders of days gone by are becoming few and far between.

Chapter Seven

Ingram-Richardson, A Photo Essay

This chapter is dedicated to the memory and historical significance of the Ingram-Richardson Corporation. Founded by Louis Ingram and Ernest Richardson, it began operations in 1901 and its long and prolific career ended on July 29, 1967. It was the largest porcelain manufacturer in the United States and at one time employed close to a thousand people. Its 162,000 square foot complex was situated in the beautiful mountain setting of Beaver Falls, Pennsylvania. Although Ingram-Richardson was founded as a manufacturer of high-quality advertising signs, they were also the first in the United States to produce porcelain enamel table tops as well as decorated breakfast sets, refrigerator linings, and gas heaters. They also produced laundry tub covers and drain boards for sinks. In 1911, Ing-Rich produced the first completely porcelain enamel gas kitchen range. In later years, the manufacture of architectural porcelain enamel building panels became a mainstay of their production line. Many of the spectacular items presented in this chapter are courtesy of Ingram-Richardson's great grandson, Jeffery Ingram Sherill.

This rectangular serving tray was produced by Ingram-Richardson in the 1920s. It features a colorful nature motif; approximately 17" x 12".

This tray is made of inorganic porcelain enamel fused above 1500° F. to enameling quality steel. The design is applied by the silk screen process.

Ingram-Richardson Mfg. Co.
Beaver Falls, Pa.

This silk-screened information was applied to the back of the tray and not only identified the tray's manufacturer, but gave the consumer an idea as to its virtues.

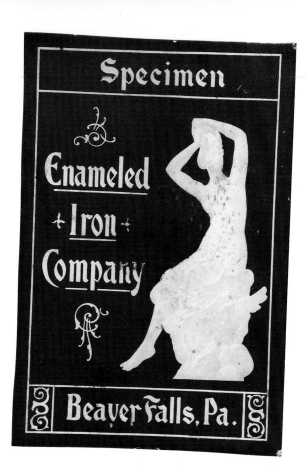

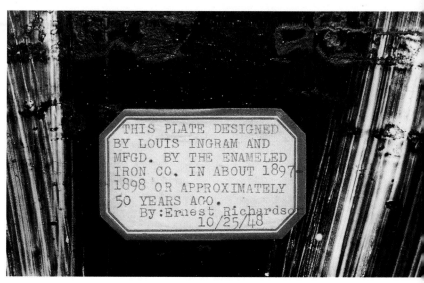

This decal is attached to the back of the Specimen sign. Notice the crude grip coat of black porcelain applied to the steel.

The Enameled Iron Company employed Ernest Richardson in the late 1800s. This early advertising piece was made around 1897-1898; 8" x 14".

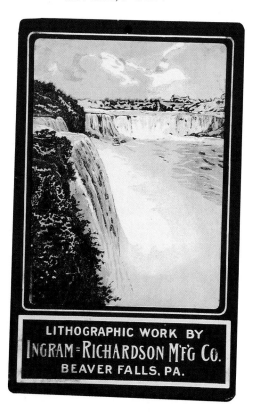

This gorgeous advertisement for lithographic work was manufactured by Ingram-Richardson sometime around 1910; 8" x 16".

Ingram-Richardson was one of the largest manufacturers in the Beaver Falls, Pennsylvania, area. An annual banquet for the manufacturers association was held in Beaver County and this porcelainized plate was a part of their June 16, 1911 annual celebration. The association's speakers and members as well as the dinner menu sheets were all originally attached to the sign.

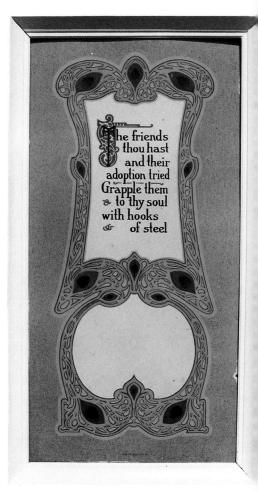

This poetic example of the early use of porcelain enamel was done by Ingram-Richardson around 1907; 20" x 36".

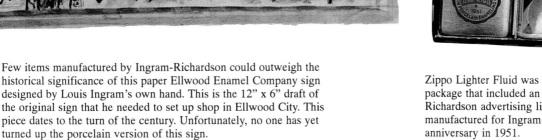

Few items manufactured by Ingram-Richardson could outweigh the historical significance of this paper Ellwood Enamel Company sign designed by Louis Ingram's own hand. This is the 12" x 6" draft of the original sign that he needed to set up shop in Ellwood City. This piece dates to the turn of the century. Unfortunately, no one has yet turned up the porcelain version of this sign.

Zippo Lighter Fluid was in this small-sized package that included an Ingram-Richardson advertising lighter. These were manufactured for Ingram-Richardson's 50th anniversary in 1951.

Enameled Iron Signs are advertised on this 10" x 14" specimen dating to the late 1800s.

Ingram-Richardson manufactured thousands of plates through the years. This copper plate is shown from the back to highlight the Porceliron decal presented here; 3" x 8".

Although somewhat difficult to read, this Ingram-Richardson letter opener advertised their company's signs; 1.5" x 6".

Thomas Edison is pictured on this Enameled Iron Company specimen dating somewhere in the late 1800s; 6" x 8".

These two 4" diameter trivets were manufactured by Ingram-Richardson to help advertise their Frankfort, Indiana, and Bayonne, New Jersey, operations.

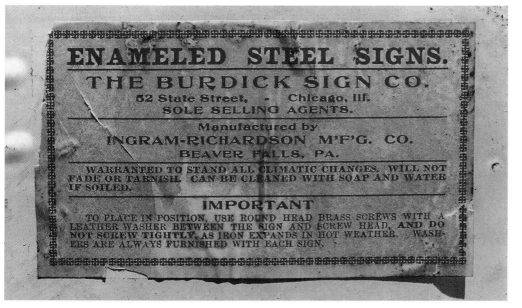

The four photographs presented here represent ways that Ingram-Richardson marked the reverse side of their porcelain enamel products. As you can see, their representative for distribution and sales was on two of the Burdick Sign Company decals.

144

This early sketch of the Ing-Rich plant going full force was made by the Luck Company of Cleveland, Ohio, in 1914. As you can see, Ing-Rich's operation was busy place indeed!

Now Celebrating the
50th Anniversary
OF OUR FOUNDING

OPEN HOUSE

AT OUR PLANT

*Friday
June 22*

1 to 9 p.m.

Louis Ingram

Ernest Richardson

Fifty years ago Ingram-Richardson Manufacturing Company was established in Beaver Falls. The company developed from the dreams and sound planning of two men—Louis Ingram and Ernest Richardson. One of the pioneers in the infant porcelain enameling industry, this local organization prospered, and grew, and today occupies a position of leadership in its field. Originally Ing-Rich was exclusively a producer of porcelain enameled signs, but through the years, porcelain enamel production know-how led to the development of many additional products. Ing-Rich was the first to manufacture porcelain enameled table tops, breakfast sets, refrigerator linings, gas heaters, gas kitchen ranges and drain boards for sinks. The company also was a pioneer producer of architectural porcelain enamel.

You are Invited . . . to an Open House at our plant to help us celebrate our 50th birthday. Time: 1 p.m. until 9 p.m. on Friday, June 22.

A Word About Some ING-RICH *People*

Ing-Rich's 50 years of steady progress is directly traceable to the sincere good will and cooperation of the men and women who have worked there. In good times and in bad the company's success depends directly upon Ing-Rich people. Many men and women have contributed much of their lives to working for the company. We'd particularly like to salute the following employees who have served for 25 years or more.

B. F. Carothers	Louis Puchleitner	Frank Deselich	Ralph Main	Jos. Godulae	John Hornacek	Wm. Landsbach
Charles Frederick	Thomas Frederick	Margaret A. Littell	Angelo Pisano	Joseph Schurkee	Martin Sebaly	Jacob Hribnak
J. H. E. McMillan	Earl Stanyard	Howard Romigh	John Kwietnewski	James Harter	Wm. Vanner	Victor Neff
William Schuler	James Pasarilla	Nick Gregovich	Fern Ridings	Andy Brozko	Howard K. Yoho	Frank Muzzi
Harry McClane	Ralph Frederick	John Koscan	Claude Thompson	Mike Kabot	David L. Brooks	George A. Rozich
Joseph Rolinson	John Rayz	George Neumont	Frank Bell	Jacob Bobin	Ethel Stanyard	Wm. Braheny
William J. Tress	Lewis Johnson	John Brozech	James Crichton	Mike Oravitz	Earl Tate	Paul Kruty
Agnes L. Strub	George Terdick	Dealva D. Crumrine	John Magee	Wm. George	Albert Dainton	John Horstman
Samuel J. Frederick	Harry Stanyard	Jas. G. Bittner	George Schuler	Mike Kaszonyi	Ira Conley	Mike Majcher
George Wachter	Anthony Schnubel	James Soriano	Herman C. Schuler	John Toth	Mike Lukacs	Edward Kraft
John Steiner	George Margea	Frank Barti	Pete Deselich	Frank Morelli	Anthony Sobiecky	Matthew C. Dainton
Bess L. Demorest						Clarence Yoho

INGRAM-RICHARDSON MANUFACTURING COMPANY

BEAVER FALLS, PENNSYLVANIA

MAKERS OF: Porcelain Enameled Signs and Table Tops, Architectural Porcelain Enamel, Custom Enameled Products and Specialties

Friday, June 22, was a big day for Ingram-Richardson, as seen in this 14" x 23" poster.

Ingram-Richardson distributed many promotional pamphlets through the years. This one from the early 1950s outlined the many advantages of porcelain enamel advertising.

These photographs represent operations inside of the Ing-Rich factory. They were photographed sometime in the 1930s and depict some of the processes involved in the manufacture of porcelain enamel advertising. Notice such details as the lack of safety precautions by the gentleman spraying the large Shell sign and the very collectible goodie hanging upside down on the conveyor rack getting ready to be fired at 1,700 degrees. These large furnaces utilized a conveyor system that extended hundreds of feet and took the signs not only through the furnaces but to some of the other operational points in the plant as well.

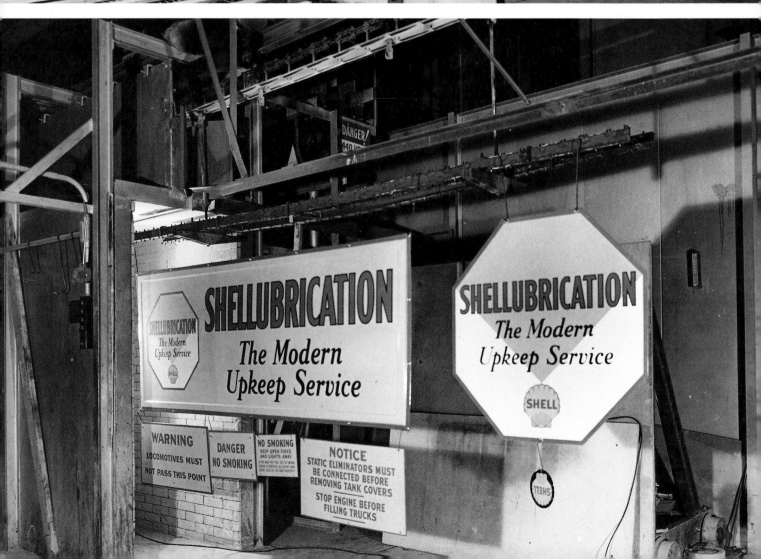

For the New

RCA Offices and Laboratories (Cherry Hill Project)

Architect: Vincent G. Kling, Philadelphia   *General Contractor:* Turner Construction Company

ING-RICH
PORCELPANELS®

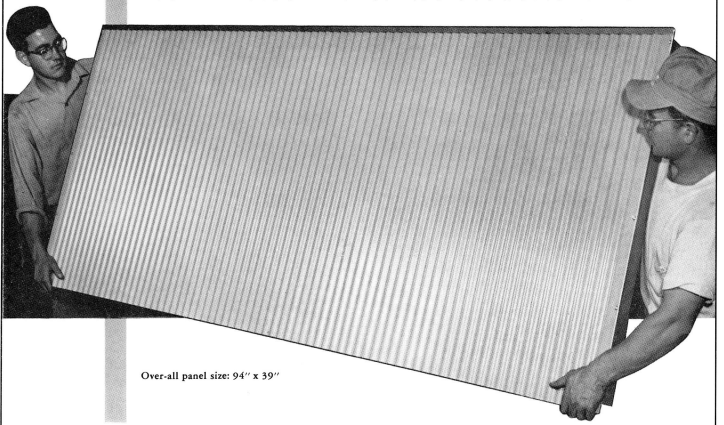

Over-all panel size: 94" x 39"

The description on the following pages is abstracted from an article
appearing in the July 1954 issue of ARCHITECTURAL RECORD

INGRAM-RICHARDSON MANUFACTURING COMPANY
BEAVER FALLS, PA.
Member, Architectural Division, Porcelain Enamel Institute

These two gentlemen are holding one of the Porcelpanels developed by
Ingram-Richardson in the 1950s. These were used on many large buildings
through the years as an attractive alternative for building exteriors.

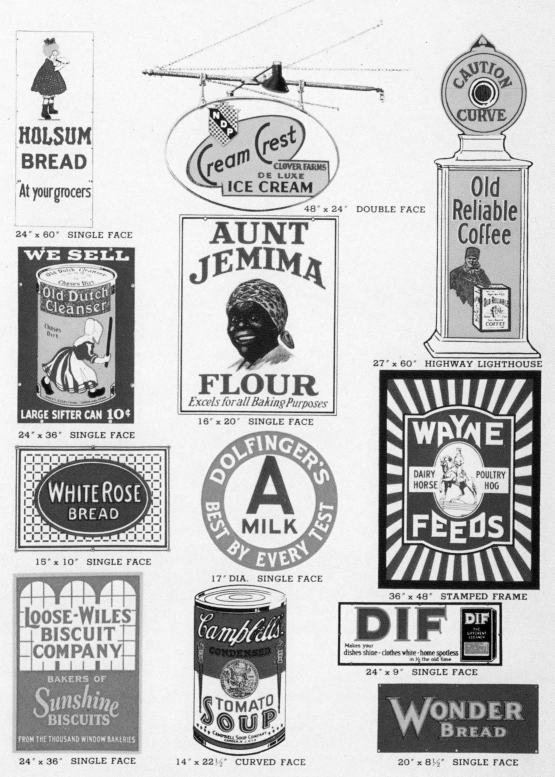

HOLSUM BREAD "At your grocers"
24" x 60" SINGLE FACE

Cream Crest CLOVER FARMS DE LUXE ICE CREAM
48" x 24" DOUBLE FACE

WE SELL Old Dutch Cleanser LARGE SIFTER CAN 10¢
24" x 36" SINGLE FACE

AUNT JEMIMA FLOUR Excels for all Baking Purposes
16" x 20" SINGLE FACE

CAUTION CURVE Old Reliable Coffee
27" x 60" HIGHWAY LIGHTHOUSE

WHITE ROSE BREAD
15" x 10" SINGLE FACE

DOLFINGER'S A MILK BEST BY EVERY TEST
17" DIA. SINGLE FACE

WAYNE FEEDS DAIRY HORSE POULTRY HOG
36" x 48" STAMPED FRAME

LOOSE-WILES BISCUIT COMPANY BAKERS OF Sunshine BISCUITS FROM THE THOUSAND WINDOW BAKERIES
24" x 36" SINGLE FACE

Campbell's CONDENSED TOMATO SOUP
14" x 22½" CURVED FACE

DIF Makes your dishes shine · clothes white · home spotless in ½ the old time
24" x 9" SINGLE FACE

WONDER BREAD
20" x 8½" SINGLE FACE

Your own grocery store probably displays at least one Ing-Rich Sign installed by some far-seeing manufacturer.

D-2

152

DEVOE
PAINTS
25" x 47" DOUBLE FACE BRACKET

BYERS BEAR CAT CRANE
20" DIA. SINGLE FACE

GLIDDEN PAINTS
AUTHORIZED DEALER
36" x 20"
DOUBLE FACE BRACKET

Pee Gee PAINTS
20" x 14" DOUBLE FACE FLANGE

Lawrence
TIGER BRAND
PAINT & VARNISH
F. P. COLLINS PAINT CO., INC.
225 W. FAYETTE ST. SYRACUSE. N.Y.
70" x 42"   70" x 14"

AUTHORIZED DEALER
PLEXITE
SAFETY GLASS
AMERICAN WINDOW GLASS CO.
24" x 14" DOUBLE FACE BRACKET

Diavolo Coals
Produced by The Colorado Fuel and Iron Company
SOLD HERE
24" x 20" SINGLE FACE

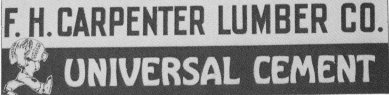

F. H. CARPENTER LUMBER CO.
UNIVERSAL CEMENT
96" x 24" SINGLE FACE—IMPRINTED

Dealers' stores, distributors' yards, the hauling and handling equipment and even the location of the job carry identification by Ing-Rich.

B-2

153

Famous National Signs

THESE are just *a few* of the Signs we have made for National Advertisers. Yet there are enough shown here to prove the superiority of the Ing-Rich Sign. Signs are an investment. Their only value is their sales value. To post an entire nation involves a great deal of money. You may rest assured that these advertisers would *NOT* use Ing-Rich Signs if some other Sign returned a higher dividend on the investment.

16

Made by Ingram-Richardson

SIGNS like these make strong dealers out of weak ones, and stronger dealers out of strong ones. There is no doubt of that. Once more these pages prove it. These manufacturers, representing the keenest business brains of the age, would not spend Millions for Signs if Signs were not unquestionably profitable. And they are just as profitable to the concern of local scope as to the National Advertiser.

17

Guaranteed not to rust, fade or tarnish for a period of ten years

12

If you want to advertise to everybody, put your Signs outside

21

ING-RICH
SIGNS

for

Street & Traction

Guaranteed not to rust, fade or tarnish for ten years

YOU, the Street Commissioner or Traction Executive, can render the public a far better service and at the same time save much money by the adoption of Ing-Rich Signs.

How long do your painted or lithographed Signs last? *Seldom more than a year.* Are they readable? *The older ones are not.* How long do Ing-Rich Signs last? *Ten Years, under guarantee—usually much longer.* What do they cost? *Far less, in the end, than ordinary Signs.*

Aside from service and economy, appearance should be thought of. A forlorn apology of a Sign ruins the appearance of an otherwise handsome car. Clean-cut Street, Traffic and Ordinance Signs help, rather than hurt, the appearance of your streets. Progressive cities, towns and traction companies from Maine to California are using Ing-Rich Signs. Why don't you?

22

As conspicuous on the crowded street as a billboard in a lonely field

11

ING-RICH
SIGNS

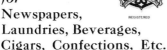

for

Newspapers,
Laundries, Beverages,
Cigars, Confections, Etc.

Guaranteed not to rust, fade or tarnish for ten years

HERE is a difficulty that every user of "cheap" Signs encounters. No matter how pretty they may be at first sight, the dealer knows that in a few months they will be *wrecks*. Because he takes pride in the appearance of his building, permission to put them up is *justly refused*. And the better the store—in other words, *the more valuable the location*—the greater the difficulty.

It is rare indeed that an Ing-Rich Sign is refused. *Ninety-nine times out of a hundred they GO UP.* Moreover, in view of their ten-year guarantee, they cost you much less money—for the Signs themselves and for putting them up.

18

THE FLANGED COLLAR around the hole prevents the screw head from coming in contact with the enamel surface. This not alone does away with the washer but, most important of all, keeps the enamel from chipping around the screw hole.

On the job, at full efficiency, every day for ten years or longer

15

POLARINE OIL AND GREASES FOR MOTOR CARS

Lettered Both Sides, 20"x9"

Door Plate
4"x11"

WE SELL SO-CO-NY MOTOR GASOLINE STANDARD OIL CO. OF N.Y.

Lettered Both Sides, 20"x24"

MOTOR VALVOLINE OILS

Lettered Both Sides, 16"x10"

GASOLINE Fisk Tires AUTO SUPPLIES

Lettered Both Sides, 24"x18"

GARAGE Firestone TIRES GASOLINE

Lettered Both Sides, 21"x16"

GOODRICH AUTOMOBILE TIRES SOLD HERE

Lettered Both Sides, 18" Circle

GARGOYLE Mobiloil VACUUM OIL COMPANY Rochester, U.S.A.

Lettered Both Sides, 20"x14"

"WAVERLY" OILS AND GASOLINE

Lettered Both Sides, 16"x10"

A little higher first cost—a tremendously lower last cost

14

CHEW SMOKE MAIL POUCH TREAT YOURSELF TO THE BEST

Lettered One Side, 36"x11"

BAYUK BROS HAVANA RIBBON 5¢ CIGAR

Lettered Both Sides, 18"x13½"

NORTH STAR CHOCOLATES

Lettered One Side, 36"x4"

Huylers BONBONS CHOCOLATES

Lettered One Side, 30"x10"

PENCO

Lettered One Side, 14½"x2"

Piedmont "THE CIGARETTE OF QUALITY"

Lettered One Side, 36"x13"

Tom Keene CIGAR

Lettered Both Sides, 18"x18"

EISENLOHR'S Cinco CIGARS

Lettered Both Sides, 17"x13"

Signs like these are a powerful hook-up between advertising and sales

19

EAGLE LAUNDRY

Lettered Both Sides, 20"x10"

AGENCY GLOBE LAUNDRY BUNDLES CALLED FOR DAILY

Lettered One Side, 18"x12"

WORLD ADVTG WANT AGENCY

Lettered Both Sides, 18"x8"

Pilgrim Laundering Co.

Lettered One Side, 35"x21"

The Louisville Evening Post KENTUCKY'S GREATEST NEWSPAPER TODAYS NEWS TODAY FOR SALE HERE

Drum Sign, 15"x22"

AGENCY PERRY'S LAUNDRY CO.

Lettered One Side, 30"x6"

TROY TIMES ART SECTION EVERY SATURDAY

Lettered Both Sides, 16"x8"

GLOBE STEAM LAUNDRY AGENCY

Lettered Both Sides, 16"x9"

If you want to advertise to the few—use Indoor Signs

20

ING-RICH SIGNS *for* Automobile Tires, Supplies, Tools, Etc.

Guaranteed not to rust, fade or tarnish for ten years

MANY products have traveled to fame via the Billboard. But if you make your appeal through Billboards—*and then stop*—you do NOT get maximum returns for your money.

Nail your Billboards to your agencies by means of Ing-Rich Signs. Dealer's Outdoor Signs are seen by *thousands* to every *hundred* who see a Billboard. They are seen *at the place of sale*, where *immediate action* is possible, instead of in the suburbs or the country. They cost as many *cents* as your Billboards cost *dollars*, and for space and maintenance *not one cent*.

13

AGENCY FOR *Washusett* SHIRTS

Lettered Both Sides, 14"x10"

AGENCY HARTFORD FIRE INS. CO.

Lettered Both Sides, 18"x12"

Best Quality   Best Value
PIANOS
THE CABLE COMPANY
ATLANTA

Drum, 16"x10"

DUTCHESS TROUSERS
10 Cents a Button
$1.00 a Rip

Lettered Both Sides, 16"x9"

WEAR GOTHAM HATS

Lettered One Side, 14" Circle

The EDISON PHONOGRAPH

Lettered One Side, 16"x7"

LADIES HOME JOURNAL PATTERNS

Lettered Both Sides, 20"x10"

EAGLE SHIRTS

Lettered One Side, 23¼"x3¼"

Guaranteed not to rust, fade or tarnish for a period of ten years

10

ING-RICH SIGNS
for
Factories,
Safety First and Display

Guaranted not to rust, fade or tarnish for ten years

BY the aid of Safety First Signs it is possible to tell every employee of your plant everything that safety requires him to know, and to make it practically impossible for him to forget.

In the steam, grime and fumes of the average mill, painted or lithographed Signs endure only a few months. But Ing-Rich Signs, heavily enameled on both sides, are guaranteed to resist all damage from these agencies for a period of ten years. They are always clean and legible. And in the end they are enormously cheaper.

The same. is true of Ing-Rich Signs as applied to the big, outside display of your factory name. Does *your* factory have a name?

25

ING-RICH SIGNS
for
Clothing,
Shoes, Hats, Shirts, Etc.

Guaranteed not to rust, fade or tarnish for ten years

IN any line of business, Dealer's Outdoor Signs are immeasurably superior to Indoor Signs. The reason is immediately apparent. Outdoor Signs are seen by *every man and woman who walks the street;* Indoor Signs, only by the few who enter the store. Even these are intent upon their purchasing.

Use Outdoor Signs for identically the same reason that you prefer the Magazine or Newspaper of wide circulation. Use Ing-Rich Signs because, with them, you can secure in permanent form all the bold strength, dainty effect or complex design possible to Indoor Signs, and *place it where ALL will see.*

7

BEACON SHOE
WE ARE EXCLUSIVE AGENTS FOR
BEACON SHOES

Lettered Both Sides, 18"x12"

Kuppenheimers GUARANTEED CLOTHING

Drum, 20"x14"

LONG WEAR SHOES
CRADDOCK-TERRY CO.

Lettered Both Sides. For Hanger, 16"x17"

AGENCY RADCLIFFE SHOE FOR WOMEN

Drum, 14"x18".   Mahogany Finish

TAYLOR WILL TAILOR IT RIGHT

Flange Sign, 20½"x10"

PERFECT FIT
MADE TO MEASURE
INTERNATIONAL CLOTHES
POPULAR PRICES

Lettered Both Sides
21"x17"

EDUCATOR SHOE
Lets the childs foot grow as it should
RICE & HUTCHINS MAKERS BOSTON

Drum, 12"x18"

WE SELL
LION BRAND
TRADE MARK
CLOTHING

Drum, 18"x13".   Golden Oak Finish

Permission to put up Signs like these is almost never refused

9

This aerial view of Ingram-Richardson's operations was taken
sometime around World War II.

Parting Shots

The beautiful western motif created here *expresses* the interests of Bill and Belinda Fraser.

If you're looking for an eye full, check out this panorama from the home of Lee and Bonnie Kollorz. Not only do they collect porcelain enamel, but have secured a beautiful assortment of early Americana as well.

You never know what you'll find at 8,000 feet above sea level. The assortment of porcelain presented here is one of many to be found in the home of John Bobroff.

Hunta, Ontario, is home to the Museum of Days Gone By. This remote location is worth a visit. It contains hundreds of artifacts from the early automotive and farming days. One of the buildings in the complex is presented here with a large White Rose porcelain sign prominently placed outside. The museum is operated by Jerry and Phyllis Miller.

These petro signs adorn the living room of Dave and Kathy Lane.

A large pole barn was built to contain the collection of John Romagnoli. Although only part of it is pictured here, similar goodies can be found on the other walls as well.